India's Policy in the United Nations

India's Policy in the United Nations

T. Ramakrishna Reddy

Rutherford • Madison • Teaneck
Fairleigh Dickinson University Press

Library of Congress Catalogue Card Number: 67–26816

Associated University Presses, Inc.
Cranbury, New Jersey 08512

6755
Printed in the United States of America

to my mother

Acknowledgments

Acknowledgments

In writing this study, the author greatly benefited from the perceptive criticism and helpful suggestions of Dr. Richard Butwell. He is deeply grateful to Dr. Butwell, who, as Direc-tor of the present study, provided valuable guidance and was most generous with his time. Special thanks are due to Dr. Amry Vandenbosch, former Director of the Andrew Patter-son School of Diplomacy and International Commerce of the University of Kentucky, for his provocative and stimulating encouragement to the author in undertaking the present study. The author wishes to acknowledge the helpful advice and the keen interest shown in the project by professors Malcolm E. Jewell and Herbert A. Drennon.

The author is indebted to the Department of Political Science and the School of Diplomacy of the University of Kentucky for making available the financial grants so neces-sary for completing the project. He sincerely appreciates the help of the Margaret I. King Library of the University of Kentucky in providing the needed research data through their Inter-Library Loan System. A word of thanks is due to the Library of Congress and to the Permanent Mission of the

Government of India at the United Nations Headquarters for providing valuable information on the project.

Finally, the author appreciates Mrs. Bee Werner for her conscientiousness at the typewriter.

Contents

Contents

Introduction

The objective of the present study is to examine India's policy toward various political, security and organizational issues in which India has taken a special interest at the United Nations. The study is not concerned with all aspects of India's policy. It proposes to consider India's conception of the United Nations, attitude toward amending the United Nations Charter, colonialism, the United Nations peace-keeping forces, financing the United Nations, and the Organization's Secretariat. The focus of the study is the General Assembly and its main committees.

India's policy toward major issues at the United Nations is of particular interest. It is worthy of consideration because it has a bearing on the policies of the Afro-Asian countries. India, for instance, has been a leading advocate of non-alignment and a prominent critic of colonialism. India has given direction and leadership to the Afro-Asians on these questions and on many issues that have come before the United Nations. India's policy is not an isolated phenomenon but operates in the general context of world politics. India's

position in the Afro-Asian world, her influence among the
non-aligned states, her size, and her geographic position,
make her an important member of the United Nations. Since
India's influence among the new states is considerable, it is
essential to understand what India's policy is and why that
policy today is what it is.

The study examines the factors conditioning Indian foreign policy in relation to the United Nations. The aim is to
study the factors inspiring the policy and India's perception
of how her policy goals could be and should be achieved.
One central factor in India's policy is the pervading Indian
desire for recognition of her position in world affairs and her
attempts to enhance her position at the United Nations. The
study revolves around the hypothesis that India's desire for
recognition led her to participate actively in the United Nations. Around this hypothesis several propositions are built
to examine the relationship between India's participation in,
and her utilization of, the United Nations in implementing
her policy objectives. In the course of examination it will be
shown that India's successful utilization of the United Nations stirred her to support the Organization.

In the course of the study, it will become obvious that
certain propositions are invalid. The study aims to dispel
some of the misconceptions on India's attitude toward colonialism. In 1958 while considering India's anti-colonial role
in the United Nations, Ross N. Berkes and Mohinder S. Bedi
pointed out "the uneven beginnings in the transformation of
India's performance from that of a radical power to that of a
conservative power."[1] They remarked that there was, in
India's policy, "evidence of a growing cautiousness on colonial issues."[2] The author almost believed their conclusion

[1] Ross N. Berkes, Mohinder S. Bedi, *The Diplomacy of India: Indian
Foreign Policy in the United Nations* (Stanford: Stanford University
Press, 1958), p. 203.
[2] *Ibid.*, p. 195.

that India has moved from an aggressive role to a role of moderation on colonial questions. However, a perusal of the statements by Indian leaders and her delegates at the United Nations on colonial issues during the past two decades revealed the invalidity of the Berkes and Bedi conclusions. An effort is made to show that India is neither a conservative nor a radical power, but simply an Indian power which maintained basically a consistent position toward colonialism. The study proposes to present the perennial existence of both extremism and moderation in India's anti-colonialism. It is shown in the study that there is a reciprocative factor in India's anti-colonial policy. India's assumption of a moderate position over various colonial issues in the early stages of the United Nations history and her adoption of an intransigent posture toward certain colonial questions is strikingly presented in the paper.

The scheme of this study is the presentation and evaluation of India's foreign policy. There is no attempt to either justify or condemn the policy of the Government of India. The most permeating factor in India's policy, on issues considered under this study, is her desire to promote her national interest. Kashmir, for instance, loomed large whenever the question of establishing United Nations peace-keeping forces was considered. Besides self-interest, various factors such as the low level of India's economic development, the impact of idealism and the influence of political ideology are taken into consideration in evaluating India's policy. Believing that a knowledge of the basic objectives of India's foreign policy and her conception of the United Nations is essential for an understanding of India's policy at the United Nations, an attempt is made to present India's policy objectives and her view of the United Nations.

The study considers the past and present positions that India has adopted in her participation in the United Nations. Needless to say, a grasp of the tendencies and continuities

which emerge from the past is essential to understand the
present and to assert the course that the policy would follow
in the future. The author aims to show that what appears to
be a contradictory attitude of India toward the issues under
consideration is not, in fact, illogical. There is broad support
for the policy pursued by the Government of India at the
United Nations. Since her independence in 1947, India has
been under a single political party and until May, 1964 she
was under the hegemony of Prime Minister Jawaharlal
Nehru. It is pointed out in the study that the old foreign
policy of Mr. Nehru, with regard to the United Nations,
tends to persist in India's thinking, particularly under the
present leadership of Mrs. Indira Gandhi.

It is hoped that the present study will stimulate further research on the subject. An empirical study could be conducted, for instance, on the extent of India's satisfaction
with, and the degree of her support to, the United Nations.
The study provides new and valuable dimensions on India's
anti-colonial policy at the United Nations. Interviews with
India's policy-makers would enable a researcher to measure
the extent of their abhorrence or appreciation of a colonial
policy and the degree of their antipathy or sympathy toward
that policy.

With regard to sources, the main emphasis is placed on the
Official Records of the General Assembly and its main committees. For Indian official statements outside the United
Nations, the study primarily depends on the *Indian Parliamentary Debates*. In the examination of the nature and content of Indian foreign policy, the major reliance is placed on
various secondary sources. The chief sources of information
on current events and on recent policy statements by Indian
statesmen are *The New York Times, The Times,* London,
and *The Hindu Weekly Review*.

India's Policy in the United Nations

1

India's Conception
of the United Nations

India viewed the United Nations as an international organization of sovereign states with different social, political and
economic systems and not as an exclusive club of a power
bloc in the cold war. According to Mrs. Vijayalakshmi
Pandit the United Nations "has no 'ism' of its own; it embraces all 'isms' and ideologies; it embraces all civilizations
of the West and of the East; its principles cannot be said to
derive exclusively from either or any of the contending doc-
trines."[1] India's conception of the United Nations had been
characterized by her advocacy of admission to all states that
satisfy charter provisions, by her resistance to the domination

[1] United Nations, General Assembly, Second Session, *Official Records,*
Vol. 11, 85th plenary meeting (17 September 1947) (New York, 1948),
p. 138.

of the United Nations by a bloc of powers and by her attempts to broaden the United Nations in a way that would represent the realities of the world.

UNIVERSALITY OF MEMBERSHIP

India championed the principle of universality and strove to promote the universal character of the United Nations by advocating "a liberal interpretation of charter provisions with respect to the admission of all new members."[2] India favored the admission of all states into the United Nations, "irrespective of differences in regimes or policies,"[3] in order to broaden "the universal character of the international organization."[4] Mr. V. K. Krishna Menon, urging the enlargement of the membership of the United Nations, pointed out that "the founding fathers thought in terms not merely of having some nice people here, but of having the world as it is."[5] Sir B. N. Rau argued that "refusing admission to peace loving and sovereign states on grounds which had nothing to do with the merits of their applications would be disastrous both for the organization's prestige and author-

---

[2] Shanti Narayan Varma, "India's Policy in the United Nations with respect to the maintenance of International Peace and Security" (unpublished Ph.D. dissertation, Department of Political Science, Columbia University), p. 49. See also United Nations, General Assembly, Third Session, part 1, *Official Records, Ad Hoc* political committee, ninth meeting (23 November 1948) (Paris, 1948), p. 89.

[3] "India and Twenty Years of UN," *India News*, July 23, 1964, p. 5. See also Hector Abhayavardhan "The United Nations, A Symposium on its Organization and Future" *Seminar* (March 1962), p. 13.

[4] K. P. Karunakaran, *India in World Affairs 1950-53* (London: Oxford University Press, 1958) p. 141. See also *The New York Times,* June 15, 1953, p. 8.

[5] United Nations, General Assembly, Fourteenth Session, *Official Records,* 803rd plenary meeting, agenda item 8 (A/4222, 22 September 1959) (New York, 1960), p. 93. See also J. A. Naik "India in the World Affairs," *United Asia,* Vol. 16 (July-August 1964), p. 230.

ity."[6] Prime Minister Jawaharlal Nehru, disapproving a proposal that aimed to limit the membership of the United Nations, said that the proposal surprised him greatly and it seemed to "forget the very purpose and the very nature of the United Nations."[7] In 1955 the efforts of the Indian delegation at New York and Mr. Nehru's talks with the Russian leaders at Delhi were crucial in breaking the deadlock over admission of new members into the United Nations.[8] Menon stated that "the strengths and the capacity of the United Nations to implement the purposes of the charter largely depend upon the loyalty it can command of all the peoples of the world."[9] He warned that limiting the membership of the United Nations would endanger the position of the organization. He explained that "the last few years have shown that whenever a problem of some importance, as some representatives have said, has arisen, then another forum and another universe of discourse has to be found somewhere and other platforms have to be created. The United Nations will be reduced to a position that whenever any important matter

[6] "Asia's Coming of Age," *United Nations Bulletin,* Vol. 7, No. 7 (October 1, 1949), p. 365. Mr. Rau said that no irrelevant consideration should bar the admission of a state satisfying the provisions of the charter. *Ibid.* See also United Nations, General Assembly, Sixth Session, *Official Records,* 344th plenary meeting, agenda item 8 (14 November 1951) (Paris, 1952), p. 129, and United Nations, General Assembly, Tenth Session, *Official Records,* 533rd plenary meeting, agenda item 9 (4 October 1955) (New York, 1955), p. 234.

[7] Jawaharlal Nehru, *India's Foreign Policy:* Selected Speeches September 1946-April 1961 (New Delhi: Publications Division, Ministry of Information and Broadcasting, Government of India, 1961), p. 167.

[8] Arthur Lall, "Change and Continuity in India's Foreign Policy," *Orbis,* "Quarterly Journal of World Affairs," published by the Foreign Policy Research Institute of the University of Pennsylvania, Vol. X, No. 1 (Spring, 1966), p. 100.

[9] United Nations, General Assembly, Tenth Session, *Official Records,* 580th plenary meeting, agenda item 8, (16 November 1956) (New York, 1957), p. 76. See also K. P. Karunakaran, "India and the United Nations," *The March of India,* Vol. X, No. 10 October, 1958), p. 9.

comes up, it must be discussed somewhere else."[10] This idea was restated by President Sarvepalli Radhakrishnan in 1963 when he said universality would make possible the implementation of United Nations decisions by all nations.[11]

Mr. Menon complained that instead of a family of nations the United Nations was being made an exclusive club in which one group was trying to exclude the candidates of another group and thus to maintain an Assembly of like-minded members.[12] India maintained that the United Nations should reflect the realities of the world and for such a purpose, it should include all independent states satisfying conditions for membership. A study on *India and the United Nations* concluded that India's aim had been to make it an organization which would "reflect the existing political and military realities of the international situation."[13]

Mr. V. K. Krishna Menon argued that all states satisfying the conditions laid down in the charter should be admitted into the United Nations, although they differed ideologically from one another, for they could make a useful contribution to the work of the United Nations. He thought that "their very opposition would then become manifest and would render the debates more fruitful because the opposing argu-

[10] United Nations, General Assembly, Fourteenth Session, *Official Records,* 803rd plenary meeting (22 September, 1959) (New York, 1959), p. 94.

[11] United Nations, General Assembly, Fourth Special Session, *Official Records,* 1204th plenary meeting (10 June 1963) (New York, 1964), p. 12.

[12] United Nations, General Assembly, Eighth Session, *Official Records,* Ad Hoc Political Committee, 12th meeting, item 22 (15 October 1953) (New York, 1953), p. 59. The same view was expressed in 1956 by Mr. Ali Yawar Jung. See United Nations, General Assembly, Twelfth Session, *Official Records,* Special Political Committee, 46th meeting, agenda item 25 (14 October 1957) (New York, 1957), p. 16.

[13] Report of a study group set up by the Indian Council of World Affairs, *India and the United Nations* (New York: Manhattan Publishing Company, 1957), p. 210. (Referred to hereafter as I.C.W.A. Study).

ments would be better known and solutions easier to find. If it was to last, the United Nations must rest on conciliation and continue to be composed of countries with ethnic and political differences."[14] Addressing the United Nations General Assembly in 1956 Mr. Nehru observed that "a forum like this, representing the world community, can deal with the problems and if not solve them at once, can positively try to solve them."[15] By attempting to find solutions the United Nations, he said, could prevent "the disastrous consequences of no solution at all."[16] The Prime Minister stated that in the world of today the United Nations was "the only hope of finding a way for peaceful cooperation among nations."[17]

Western attempts to change the essential character of the United Nations to make it an effective instrument for peace were looked upon with disdain in India. Mr. Nehru remarked that if any attempt was made to change the essential nature of the United Nations, it would not lead to "another or a more powerful organization which could work for peace."[18] Commenting on the "Uniting for Peace Resolution" Mr. Nehru made it clear that the United Nations was not an institution for implementing the policies of one bloc against another. He felt the West was converting the United Nations into a larger edition of the Atlantic Pact and making it "a war organization more than one devoted for peace." India was against a drastic change in the essential character of the United Nations for such a change would mean "the

[14] United Nations, General Assembly, Seventh Session, *Official Records,* Ad Hoc Political Committee, 47th meeting, item 19 (17 December 1952) (New York, 1953), p. 293.

[15] Nehru, *op. cit.,* p. 174.

[16] *Facts on File Yearbook, 1956,* Vol. 16, No. 843 (December 19-25, 1956), p. 429, Y-F.

[17] Nehru, *op.cit.,* p. 167.

[18] Nehru, *op. cit.,* p. 168.

exit of the soviet bloc from the United Nations."[19] To avoid such an eventuality Mr. Nehru warned that "India would quit the UN if it ousted its Communist members and that 'many' other countries would do likewise to remain neutral in the cold war."[20] The Indian Prime Minister threatened to withdraw from the United Nations to safeguard India's conception of the United Nations as a world body performing its tasks on the basis of cooperation of its members. P. P. Pillai, an Indian delegate, pointed out that the United Nations "had a positive job to perform, and in the performance of that task it must secure the cooperation of all its members."[21]

INDIA AND A BROADER UNITED NATIONS

India persistently, although cautiously, attempted to broaden the United Nations in a way that would represent the world as it was. India's resistance to the development of implementing machinery stemmed from its belief that the United Nations was dominated by the Western bloc and from its desire not to make the United Nations a tool for implementing the policies of that bloc. An observer of India's foreign policy pointed out that "it was feared in India that the forces earmarked by member states for use by the UN would not be at the disposal of the UN but at the disposal of the dominant bloc. If this happened, it would mean the death of the UN as an instrument of peaceful settlement of disputes and the emergence in its place of a global military alliance directed against a group of powers headed by the

[19] S. N. Varma, "Trends in India's Foreign Policy, 1954-57" in *Aspects of India's Foreign Policy* (prepared by the Indian Council of World Affairs, New Delhi, 1957), p. I 21.

[20] *Facts on File Yearbook, 1950,* Vol. 10, No. 497 (May 5-11, 1950), p. 147 k.

[21] "Continuance of 'Little Assembly' Recommended," *United Nations Weekly Bulletin,* Vol. 5, No. 4 (August 15, 1948), p. 630.

Soviet Union."[22] The Indian belief of Western domination of the United Nations was expressed by Mr. Nehru in 1949 when he said in the Indian Parliament that the United Nations had most of the nations in the world in it, but that it was "dominated more or less by certain great nations of Europe and America."[23] The refusal of the Security Council to hear the French-Tunisian dispute and the blocking of India from the proposed Korean Peace Conference in 1953 enhanced India's belief of Western domination.[24] A recent case in point of such domination was the skillful blocking by the Western powers of India's attempts to get the Fifteenth Session of the General Assembly to adopt a resolution calling on Premier Khrushchev and President Eisenhower to meet with each other.[25] In 1960 Nehru conceded that the United Nations had become "progressively more representative" but he contended that "even now" it was not "fully so."[26] A desire to reduce Western domination of the United Nations led India to advocate the admission of all states satisfying the provisions laid down in the charter.

India's leaders felt that the councils of the United Nations were also dominated by the West, and they attempted to minimize such an imbalance. Dr. A. R. Mudaliar complained of the over-representation of Europe and Australia in the Economic and Social Council and appealed, without

[22] Karunakaran, *op. cit.*, p. 136.

[23] Jawaharlal Nehru, *Independence and After* (New Delhi: The Publications Division, Ministry of Information and Broadcasting, Government of India, 1949), p. 251.

[24] *The Hindu,* August 30, 1953. See also *The New York Times,* April 27, 1952, p. 1, and Jawaharlal Nehru, *Jawaharlal Nehru's Speeches* 1950-53 (New Delhi: The Publications Division, Ministry of Information and Broadcasting, Government of India, 1954), p. 223.

[25] United Nations, General Assembly, Fifteenth Session, *Official Records,* 889th plenary meeting, agenda item 9 (5 October, 1960) (New York, 1961), pp. 457-469.

[26] United Nations, General Assembly, *Official Records,* 882nd plenary meeting, agenda item 9 (3 October, 1960) (New York, 1961), p. 324.

success, for a reallocation of seats. It was reported that "India favored a change in procedure in allocating seats of the ECSOC in a way to give better representation to Asia and the Middle East by reducing the over-representation of Europe and Australia."[27] Mr. Nehru argued in 1953 that there was a lack of permanent representation for Asia in the United Nations Security Council and the only representation that Asia had was through the "Chinese Nationalist Government on Formosa."[28] Both Messrs. Nehru and Menon continuously spoke of under-representation for India and Asia in the councils of the United Nations and pursued their efforts, pressing for more representation.[29]

India's policy makers contended that the admission of many new states into the United Nations resulted in a further increase of the imbalance of representation in United Nations' Councils in favor of the West and demanded a rectification of such an imbalance. According to Mr. Nehru, the structure evolved at San Francisco "was not very fair to Asia and Africa" and with many Africans coming in, the United Nations structure was "out of tune with the conditions in the world today in a variety of ways."[30] The demand for more representation in the councils of the United Nations for India and the Afro-Asians would minimize Western domination and increase India's position in the process. Mr. Nehru, proposing reforms in the United Nations structure in 1960, stated that "there was a longstanding feeling among Asian and African countries that under the present structure they

[27] Membership of Economic and Social Council, *United Nations Weekly Bulletin*, Vol. 3, No. 19 (November 4, 1947), p. 605.

[28] *The New York Times*, September 24, 1953, p. 1. See also G. L. Mehta "India in World Affairs," *Vital Speeches*, Vol. 21, No. 18 (July 1, 1955), p. 1324. The same argument could be made even today.

[29] See *The New York Times*, September 29, 1953, p. 3 and August 17, 1955, p. 15. See also "Charter Review," *United Nations Bulletin*, Vol. 16, No. 1 (January 1, 1954), p. 76.

[30] Nehru, *India's Foreign Policy, op. cit.*, p. 180, 218.

did not have the opportunity to pull their weight, and this feeling had grown stronger this year."[31]

India's attempts to reduce the Western preponderance in the United Nations councils and her efforts to increase the representation of non-Western states in those councils were met with success in 1963. The General Assembly adopted a proposal to expand the membership of the Security Council and the Economic and Social Council. The proposal, in the introduction of which the Indian delegate played an active role, aimed to give more representation to the Afro-Asians and relatively reduced distribution of seats to the European and American continents.

INDIA'S STAKES IN A BALANCED UNITED NATIONS

The admission of many non-aligned states considerably reduced Western domination over the United Nations.[32] India desired an enlargement of the independent vote (votes of non-members of the two power blocs) for "the larger the independent vote, the greater in India's opinion, might be the UN's contribution to peace."[33] A United Nations not preponderantly dominated by a single bloc would enable a state following non-alignment to maximize its influence in world affairs. Mr. Nehru was reported to have said that whenever there was a difference in the strength of two opposing forces, the Asians, with their own limitations, would not be able to influence the issue of peace, but when the two opposing

[31] *The Times,* London, October 22, 1960, p. 4.

[32] In Mr. Balaraman's view the new admissions "led to a diminution of the West's position in the Assembly" and "it no longer had the automatic two-thirds majority needed to put through decisions." See "The United Nations: A Symposium on its Organization and Future," *Seminar* (March, 1962), p. 15.

[33] Werner Levi, "Behind Nehru's Foreign Policy," *World,* Vol. 1, No. 11 (April, 1954), p. 29.

forces were fairly evenly matched, then, it would be possible "to make our weight felt in the balance."[34] In such a situation India could play the balancing role or in India's view the "bridging role."[35]

Brecher observed that "an uncommitted India can perform and has performed in some measure the necessary task of building a bridge which otherwise would not exist between two blocs."[36] The minimization of the imbalance through new admissions into the United Nations enabled India to maximize her influence in world affairs. Levi pointed out that "the political game must be played in such a manner that India in spite of her political weakness could establish a politically strategic position. This was possible, for instance, in the United Nations and other international organizations as a result of the rise of Asian and African nations to political importance. As long as their sympathy and good-will were wanted by the major powers; as long therefore as votes had more than inherent significance, India's leadership among these powers gave her political power in the international society."[37]

[34] Quoted in M. S. Rajan, "Indian Foreign Policy in Action, 1954-56." *India Quarterly*, Vol. 16 (July-September 1960), p. 233. According to Rajan only a non-aligned India could be able to tilt the balance in favor of world peace when the (two opposing forces) were evenly balanced in strength. *Ibid.*

[35] See A. Ramaswamy Mudaliar, "India's Foreign Policy" in *Nehru Abinandan Granth, A Birthday Book*. Editorial Board (Allahabad: Journal Press, 1949), p. 400.

[36] Michael Brecher, *Nehru: A Political Biography* (London: Oxford University Press, 1959), p. 559. See also T. S. Rama Rao, "India and the United Nations," in *The Indian Year Book of International Affairs 1952*, Vol. 1, ed. C. H. Alexandrowicz (Madras: University of Madras, 1952), p. 146.

[37] Werner Levi, "Necrology on Indian Neutralism," *Eastern World*, Vol. 17, No. 2 (February 1963), p. 10. Votes in the U.N. represented not only power but were treated with "moral respect." See Cyrill Falls, "Leading 'Third Force' Candidates," *The Illustrated London News*, Vol. 237 (October 8, 1960), p. 598. India's position in the Afro-Asian world although diminished, as a result of the 1962 Sino-Indian conflict, it did

Palmer expressed the view that the importance of India in world affairs was "enhanced by the nature of the existing world struggle and by India's unique and somewhat detached position with respcet to that struggle."[38] He explained that India could "hardly have enjoyed" that position and importance by "alignment with either the Soviet or Western alliance systems."[39] The United Nations provided opportunities for leadership and situations for service enabling India to further enhance her position in world affairs.[40] The wooing of the non-aligned states by the two power blocs, to achieve mathematical majorities for psychological reasons, placed India in a position far beyond the one her intrinsic power would have enabled her to achieve.[41] India's position in the non-aligned group enabled her to utilize the situation to enhance her influence. Levi pointed out that "in a cold war, for

not altogether decline. According to Norman D. Palmer, India was "still an influential member" of the Afro-Asian group in the United Nations. See Norman D. Palmer "India's position in Asia," *Journal of International Affairs,* Vol. 17, No. 2 (1962), p. 129.

[38] Norman D. Palmer, *The Indian Political System* (Boston: Houghton Mifflin Company, 1961), p. 235.

[39] Norman D. Palmer, "India's Position in Asia," p. 137. See also Mary Alice Brown, "Some Aspects of India's Foreign Policy," *United Asia,* Vol. 12, No. 6 (1960), p. 494.

[40] J. A. Naik, "India in the World Affairs," *United Asia,* Vol. 16 (July-August, 1964), p. 230.

[41] Mr. C. Rajagopalachari recognized that India's 'importance' was not as little as her 'power.' See T.M.P. Mahadevan, "India's Policy of Non-Alignment" *Indian Year Book of World Affairs, 1953,* Vol. 11, ed. C. H. Alexandrowicz (Madras: University of Madras, 1953), p. 11. A similar view was expressed by K. M. Panikkar. Mr. Panikkar believed that "given time, India had every chance to become a world power." See Karunakar Gupta, *Indian Foreign Policy: In Defense of National Interest* (Calcutta: The World Press, private Ltd, 1956), p. 74, and Robert Trumbull, *As I See India* (New York: William Sloane Associates, 1956), p. 230. It was stated that India engaged in "maximum political activity without having corresponding military power." See Philips Talbot and S. L. Poplai, *India and America* (New York: Harper and Brothers, 1958), p. 60. Mr. Nehru was conscious of it when he remarked that in spite of India's weakness in a military sense India was still counted in world affairs. Nehru, *India's Foreign Policy op. cit.,* p. 36.

instance, where propaganda and psychological warfare are important weapons, India, especially as a leader of a neutralist group, could influence the behavior of the major contestants because they cared about voting results in the United Nations."[42]

India's desire to practice non-alignment was motivated by realism as well as idealism. The objective was to increase India's influence in world affairs and at the same time to contribute to the larger objective of world peace. Mr. Nehru stated that "if we tie ourselves up with any group or bloc, a good bloc or a bad bloc, rightly or wrongly, we lose our individuality. We lose the power we have today of influencing others . . . and we just become a reflex of somebody else's mind and somebody else's activity. That seems to be from the world's point of view, a completely wrong and retrograde step for India to take."[43] He explained to the Indian Parliament in 1949 that if India were to abandon an independent policy then "we lose that tremendous vantage ground that we have of using such influence as we possess . . . in the cause of world peace."[44]

The usefulness for India of Nehru's non-alignment approach in world affairs was acknowledged by his successors.

[42] Werner Levi, "Indian Neutralism Reconsidered," *Pacific Affairs,* Vol. 37, No. 2 (Summer 1964), p. 145. The "uncommittedness" of the Afro-Asians gave them "a leverage on both Communist and major non-Communist powers" and enabled them to "exploit cold war tensions to their own advantage." See Palmer "The Afro-Asians in the UN," p. 128.

[43] Jawaharlal Nehru, *Visit to America* (New York: The John Day Company, 1950), p. 148. Nehru remarked: "As soon as we function as somebody else, our influence goes, our individuality goes and our importance goes." *Ibid,* p. 148. See also J. C. Kundra, *Indian Foreign Policy 1947-1954* (Groninzen, Netherlands, J. B. Wolters, 1955), pp. 169-170.

[44] Nehru, *India's Foreign Policy, op. cit.,* p. 39. He stated in 1960 that India's voice in the world carried some weight "not because of our army, not because of our money, but because of our policy." See *The New York Times,* January 16, 1960, p. 4. He expressed a similar view in 1962. See *Lok Sabha Debates,* Third Series, Vol. 111, No. 22 (May 14, 1962), First Session, (New Delhi: Lok Sabha Secretariat, 1962), column 4551-2.

Mr. Lal Bahadur Shastri stated that "Mr. Nehru's policy of non-alignment that had served India well in the past, and would continue to do so, would be adhered to."[45] Mr. Shastri repeated his views in a policy statement by saying that "non-alignment would continue to be the fundamental basis of India's approach to world problems."[46] Mrs. Indhira Gandhi, on becoming Prime Minister, expressed her desire to follow an independent approach in foreign affairs. She stated that "in keeping with our heritage we have followed a policy of peace and friendship with all nations, yet reserved to ourselves the right to independent opinion. The principles which have guided our foreign policy are in keeping with the best traditions of our country, and are wholly consistent with our national interest, honor and dignity. They continue to remain valid."[47] Mr. Swaran Singh, India's Foreign Minister, stated that non-alignment was a basic principle of Indian foreign policy and would continue to be so.[48]

[45] *The Times,* London, June 3, 1964, p. 10.

[46] *Ibid.* June 12, 1964, p. 12. Statesmen and scholars generally considered non-alignment as an approach—a strategy—to world affairs. Mr. Nehru viewed non-alignment as "freedom of action." See Jawaharlal Nehru, "Changing India," *Foreign Affairs,* Vol. 41, No. 3 (April 1963), p. 457. See also Nehru, *India's Foreign Policy, op. cit.,* p. 80. Mr. Krishna Menon gave a lucid exposition of the meaning of non-alignment at the 906th plenary meeting of the U.N. General Assembly. He said that India was an "unaligned and uncommitted nation in relation to the cold war." To him non-alignment was an approach and India would project her own image (internal policies) into international relations. Messrs. Rajan and Palmer considered non-alignment to be an approach. See Rajan, *op. cit.,* p. 229, and Palmer "India's Position in Asia," *op. cit.,* p. 137. Some writers argued that India viewed non-alignment as a policy. See Levi, "Necrology on Neutralism," pp. 9-11, and his "Indian Neutralism Reconsidered," pp. 137-47. See also M. Edwards, "Illusions and Reality in India's Foreign Policy," *International Affairs,* Vol. 41 (January 1965), pp. 41-48. Political scientists were perplexed to find an appropriate term that could meaningfully describe India's foreign policy. For various terms see Brecher, *op. cit.,* p. 563. Mr. Nehru preferred the term "a positive policy for peace." *Ibid.*

[47] *The Hindu Weekly Review,* January 31, 1966, p. 3.

[48] *Lok Sabha Debates,* Third Series, Vol. XXXIV, No. 15, Ninth Session (September 25, 1965) (New Delhi: Lok Sabha Secretariat, 1964),

INDIA'S DESIRE FOR INFLUENCE IN WORLD AFFAIRS

India's desire for recognition in world affairs led her to participate actively in the United Nations. India's policy at the United Nations seemed to revolve around this desire for a position in the world. Indian leaders consciously sought influence for India[49] and actively worked to corner a leading role for India in the international arena. In a historic policy statement Mr. Nehru expressed, as early as 1946, India's desire for a place in the "diplomatic sun"[50] and her intention to play a leading role in the United Nations. He enunciated that "towards the United Nations India's attitude is that of wholehearted cooperation and unreserved adherence, in both spirit and letter, to the charter governing it. To that end, India will participate fully in its various activities and endeavor to play that role in its councils to which her geographical position, population and contribution towards peaceful progress entitle her."[51] Mr. Nehru believed that various factors entitled India to play a leading role in world

---

columns 3780-1. On November 15, 1965 he repeated that "there was no need for any fundamental change in India's policy of non-alignment." See *India News*, November 26, 1965, p. 5. Arthur Lall, India's delegate to the UN for several years observed that India would "not abandon her policy of non-alignment" and that the old foreign policy of India "basically" remained intact. See Lall, "Change and Continuity in India's Foreign Policy," *Orbis*, Vol. X, No. 1 (Spring 1966), pp. 103, 105. Nehru believed in 1963 that "any government of India, would have had the same (his) policy." *Lok Sabha Debates*, Vol. XXI, No. 26, column 6622.

[49] Mr. Nehru said that one of the criteria for the pursuit of any policy was "the enhancement of the prestige of the country." See *The New York Times* November 24, 1951, p. 3.

[50] The term is borrowed from William Henderson. See William Henderson, "The roots of neutralism in Southern Asia," *Pacific Affairs*, Vol. 13, No. 1 (Winter 1957-58), p. 32.

[51] Karunakaran, *India in World Affairs 1950-53, op. cit.*, p. 236, citing *Indian Annual Register*, Vol. 2 (July-September 1946), ed. N. N. Mitra (Calcutta: N. N. Mitra, 1947), pp. 252-3.

affairs and that she could play a significant part in and out-side the United Nations. Nehru stated before the Indian Con-stituent Assembly in 1946 that by virtue of her large size and population, and of her enormous resources and her ability to exploit those resources, India could "immediately play an important and a vital part in world affairs."[52] Answering his critics in 1962 Mr. Nehru pointed out that besides bigness, in terms of size and population, "India has not only a very strong individuality; it has a long history and is a cultural entity."[53]

India's desire for recognition in world affairs stemmed from the belief of Indian leaders in India's greatness. At the time of Indian independence Nehru explained the reasons for his considering India to be a great country and the role that India should play on the world stage. He stated that "India is a great country, great in her resources, great in manpower, great in her potential, in every way. I have little doubt that a free India on every plane will play a big part on the world stage, even on the narrowest plane of material power."[54] He asserted that India would "attain its rightful

[52] Nehru, *India's Foreign Policy, op. cit.,* p. 8.
[53] *Lok Sabha Debates,* Third Series, Vol. 111, No. 22, First Session (May 14, 1962) (New Delhi: Lok Sabha Secretariat, 1962) Column 4545. Sir B. N. Rau held that India's "many religions and culture and her long and chequered history" entitled India to play an important part in world affairs. See "Asia Coming of Age," *op. cit.,* p. 364.
[54] Nehru, *India's Foreign Policy, op. cit.,* p. 13. He reiterated this con-ception often and in 1962 considered India to be a "great big country" which was "becoming a great power daily more and more." See *Lok Sabha Debates,* Third Series, Vol. 111, No. 22, First Session, (May 14, 1962) (New Delhi: Lok Sabha Secretariat, 1962), columns 4551-2. Mrs. Ghandi expressed similar views. See *Hindu Weekly Review* January 31, 1966, p. 3, Levi pointed out that the Indians felt that India was a "big power." According to Levi the Indian feeling of greatness was based, "not on India's material strength today . . . but on moral strength." See Werner Levi, "Behind Nehru's Foreign Policy," *op. cit.,* p. 25. While Mr. Nehru conceded that morality conditioned Indian foreign policy, he refuted the assumption that Indian policy was "based" on morality, see Nehru, *Independence and After, op. cit.,* p. 261.

and honored place in the world and make its full and willing contribution to the promotion of world peace and the welfare of mankind." Since the Indian policy makers considered India to be a "great country" and desired her to play "a distinctive and important role," then it was logical that they strove to make India "foremost in the arts of peace and progress."[55]

INDIA'S DESIRE FOR INFLUENCE AND NATIONALISM

A strong feeling of nationalism led Indians to consider India a great power. Brecher felt that national pride existed to astonishing proportions in India and thought that Westerners who exchanged ideas with Indians would be "struck by a pronounced feeling of national pride." He observed that "pride finds its most acute expression in the personality of Jawaharlal Nehru."[56] The content and conduct of India's foreign policy seemed to spring from a "deep inner urge for recognition." Brecher explained that "non-alignment has the added merit of satisfying a deep inner urge for recognition, a natural by-product of colonial subjection. And it enables a relatively, newly independent state to play a major role on

[55] Mr. M. Y. Kamath thought that India was "unconsciously playing the role of a Big Power." See M. Y. Kamath "India at the United Nations," *United Asia,* Vol. 9 (September 1957), p. 229.

[56] Brecher, *op. cit.,* p. 560. Sheean felt differently and doubted Mrs. Krishna Hathi Singh's view that vanity was an attribute of Nehru. However, Sheean believed that vanity existed in Menon. See Vincent Sheean, *Nehru: The Years of Power* (New York: Random House, 1960), pp. 271-2. However, Brecher's argument cannot be brushed aside. Mr. Chou-En-Lai noticed excessive pride in Nehru. This personal attribute did have an impact on policy. The following example given by Brecher would explain the relation of national and personal pride to policy: Nehru refused to sacrifice what he considered to be a measure of independence for much needed American food in 1950-51. See Brecher, *op. cit.,* p. 560. Nehru saw in his policy "the emblem of a renascent national pride." See Selig S. Harrison "Troubled India and Her Neighbors," *Foreign Affairs,* Vol. 43, No. 2 (January 1965), p. 312.

the stage of world politics."[57] The desire to plunge India into a vigorous role on the world stage was a reaction to colonial rule and to the inferior status that Indians had under colonial rule. Nair pointed out that "the international image of India had lain suppressed and distorted under imperialism in the pre-independence period. The advent of independence considerably helped these nations (like India) to rediscover their personality and to project them into the world."[58] India's independent and active role in world affairs satisfied the national sentiments of Indian leaders for it gave them a sense of pride and importance.[59]

INDIA'S ATTITUDE TOWARD NEUTRALITY

India's statesmen and diplomats made it clear that they never wanted to remain neutral in world affairs. Mr. Nehru revealed his dislike for the word "neutral" and expressed annoyance at those who called his policy "neutral."[60] Mr. Krishna Menon emphatically stated that "we are not a neutral country. We refuse to accept responsibility for the appellation 'neutralist,' which is purely a newspaper inven-

[57] *Ibid*, pp. 559-560. Mr. Rajan concurred that the desire for recognition stemmed from this inner urge for recognition. See Rajan, *op. cit.*, p. 231.

[58] N. Parameswaran Nair, "Non-Alignment, History, Ideology, Prospects," in *Outside the Contest*, ed. K. P. Karunakaran (New Delhi: Peoples Publishing House, 1963), p. 44. Nehru refused to give up his freedom and individuality. See Norman D. Palmer "Indian Attitudes Toward Colonialism," *Orbis*, Vol. 1, No. 2 (Summer 1957), pp. 230-231.

[59] N. Parameswaran Nair, "Non-Alignment in World Affairs," *India Quarterly*, Vol. 18, No. 1 (January-March 1962), p. 30. See also Norman D. Palmer "The Afro-Asians in the United Nations," in *The United States and the United Nations*. Ed Franz B. Gross (Norman: University of Oklahoma Press, 1964), p. 136. The most important factor determining India's policy was the notion of "self-respect" and the desire that India follow an independent policy of her own. See A. Appadorai "Why India believes in non-alignment," *March of India*, Vol. XIV, No. 10 (October 1962), p. 12.

[60] Nehru, *India's Foreign Policy, op. cit.*, p. 85.

tion, originally produced as an epithet by people who did not like our policy. We are not neutral as regard to war or peace. We are not neutral in regard to domination by imperialist or other countries. We are not neutral with regard to ethical values. We are not neutral with regard to the greatest economic and social problems that may arise. . . . We are not neutral or neutralist, positive or otherwise. We would take part, we would participate, we would express our views. Even that expression 'positive neutrality' is a contradiction in terms. There can no more be positive neutrality than there can be a vegetarian tiger."[61] Addressing the United States Congress in 1949, Mr. Nehru categorically stated that "where freedom is menaced, or justice threatened, or where aggression takes place, we cannot and shall not be neutral."[62]

Prime Minister Nehru conceded that India was an infant state but contended that it was an ancient country and for

[61] United Nations, General Assembly, Fifteenth Session, part 1, *Official Records,* Vol. 1, 906th plenary meeting, agenda item 9 (17 October 1960) (New York, 1961), p. 751. To Madame Pandit neutrality implied "involvement" in the cause of peace. See Vijaya Lakshmi Pandit "India's Foreign Policy," *Foreign Affairs,* Vol. 34, No. 3 (April 1956), p. 435. See also Nair "Non-Alignment, History, Ideology, Prospects," *op. cit.,* p. 44. For India, her policy implied "Something more than the mere abstention from military alliances or involvement in conflict between power blocs," see P. J. Eldridge, "India's Non-Alignment Policy Reviewed," *Australian Outlook,* Vol. 19, No. 2 (August 1965), p. 146. According to Brecher India's policy in 1947 was close to neutrality and in 1962 it had gone beyond neutralism which Nehru termed as a "positive policy for peace." Brecher makes a distinction between neutrality and neutralism. In Brecher's view neutralism was much more activist than non-alignment while neutrality was isolationist. For a discussion on these terms see Michael Brecher, "Neutralism: An Analysis," *International Journal,* Vol. 17, No. 3 (Summer 1962), pp. 224-236. To one writer non-alignment was akin to neutrality for it originally meant a refusal to join either of the two major blocs," see J. Anthony Lukas "The Non-Aligned Summit-Like Old Times," *The New York Times,* Section IV, May 15, 1966, P.5E. Mr. Anabtawi argued that a non-aligned state might "abstain totally from involvement" or might "pursue an activist policy," see Samir N. Anabtawi, "Neutralists and Neutralism," *Journal of Politics,* Vol. 27, No. 2 (May 1965), p. 357.

[62] Nehru, *Visit to America, op. cit.,* p. 144.

such a country an important role in world affairs was "inevitable." He not only ruled out a passive role for India but also rejected isolationism in world affairs. He stated that "at no time have we thought in terms of isolating ourselves in this part of the world from other countries."[63] In 1956, Mr. Nehru explained that "non-alignment does not mean passivity of mind or action, lack of faith or conviction."[64]

PURSUIT OF AN ACTIVE ROLE IN WORLD AFFAIRS

Mr. Nehru was reported to have remarked that "we cannot escape our destiny, the destiny of any great country or any great people."[65] Referring to the Geneva Conference of 1954 on Indo-China, Mr. Nehru stated that India was concerned with the deliberations of the Conference. He added that "we cannot just wash our hands of this business . . . , we cannot get away from the fact that if a situation arises which might require some kind of initiative on our part or some kind of association on our part in any particular decision, we cannot just run away and say, no, let us drift. Inevitably we cannot shed the responsibilities that go with a

[63] Nehru, *India's Foreign Policy, op. cit.,* p. 11. Professor Nair argued that "the impact of world events was mercilessly drawing them (non-aligned states) out of any policy of isolationism into which they could have otherwise taken refuge." See Nair "Non-Alignment, History, Ideology, Prospects," *op. cit.,* p. 29. This seemed to be a misconception because a country like India could have avoided an active involvement in world affairs by following a passive role but its leaders consciously chose to pursue a vigorous role. One might agree with Kundra's observation that India desired neither alignment nor isolation but chose to pursue an independent policy. See Kundra, *op. cit.,* p. 218. It was pointed out that India could not think of living in isolation. See P. S. Ramu "Policy of Non-Alignment: Has It Failed?" *AICC Economic Review,* Vol. 14 (April 15, 1963), p. 25.

[64] Quoted in Sisirranjan Saha "A Re-Appraisal of Non-Alignment" *The Calcutta Review,* Vol. 175 (April 1965), p. 20.

[65] See Rajan, *op. cit.,* p. 206. Citing *The Hindu,* Dec. 28, 1955.

great country."[66] This great power conception and the desire to get it confirmed led India to pursue an active role. Levi stated that "as a great power, albeit still in the making, India already claims the right to make her own judgments and decisions in world affairs. Indians guard this right all the more jealously since, as a newly independent state, India has not had her position in the world confirmed by history; it must be established in the years to come amid intense competition."[67] Indian leaders vigorously worked to achieve a position of importance for India in world affairs. Levi pointed out that "notwithstanding official denials for the diplomatic record of any desire for leadership or primacy in world politics, India has been pushed into a leading position,

[66] *Ibid.* He deputed Mr. Menon to render India's services in making the conference a success, although India was not one of the participants in the conference. Mr. Rosenthal observed that in 1950's Mr. Menon "became involved in the negotiations about virtually every international controversy," see A. M. Rosenthal, Krishna Menon — A Clue to Nehru," *The New York Times Magazine* (April 11, 1957), p. 69. It was reported that India was pressing to the fore in the UN and that hardly an issue arose in which the Indians didn't "actively and deeply involve themselves." See *The New York Times,* October 12, 1955, p. 7. The London *Economist* stated: "Had Mr. Khrushchev achieved his summit meeting, one country, India, would have been there, not because it had interests to defend or spheres to protect, but precisely because it had none. . . . while the great powers haggled, Mr. Nehru would have been busy broking," See "India the Uncommited," *The Economist* (August 16, 1958), p. 541.

[67] Levi, "Behind Nehru's Foreign Policy," *op. cit.,* p. 25. Some misconceptions were to be found about India's desire to play an important — "inevitable" — role. Sir B. N. Rau thought that "with its long and varied history and wide range of experiences India surely has a mission to fulfill in the present world crisis," See B. N. Rau "India and World Peace," *Nation,* Vol. 171 (December 16, 1950), p. 631. Nehru vigorously denied "any notion of a special mission for India" in the pursuit of peace. See Sheean, *op. cit.,* p. 127. Another mistaken, undoubtedly self-righteous, assumption was held by M. S. Rajan. According to him, "the government of India often felt that it had a sort of self-imposed international obligation to offer her conciliatory (not mediatory) and friendly assistance or counsel in the solution of international disputes." See Rajan, *op. cit.,* p. 218.

and her officials have assisted in the pushing."[68] Mr. Robert Trumbull stated that Nehru's delegates to the United Nations were continually striving for a stronger voice in its councils.[69] Madame Pandit considered her election as president of the General Assembly in 1953 as a recognition of India's "profound desire to serve" United Nations purposes and world peace.[70]

THE RELATIONSHIP BETWEEN THE DESIRE FOR RECOGNITION AND PARTICIPATION IN WORLD AFFAIRS

It seems that whenever a country's desire for recognition of its historic place is low then its participation in the United Nations will also be low. It might not even attempt to develop the necessary tools for such participation.[71] In recent years there was a decline in India's global aspirations. Nationhood mattered more to Mr. Shastri than global aspirations and both Mr. Shastri and Mr. Swaran Singh wanted to "contract India's role in the world."[72] Mr. Nehru himself, some years before his death, had "guided India out of the

[68] Werner Levi, "The Evolution of India's Foreign Policy," in *The Year Book of World Affairs 1958,* Vol. 12, eds. George W. Keeton and George Schwarzenberger (New York: Frederick A. Praeger, 1958), p. 116. For some Indian denials of their desire to seek leadership, see Mudaliar, *op. cit.,* p. 401. See also United Nations, General Assembly, Seventh Session, *Official Records,* First Committee, 623rd meeting, agenda item 16 (25 August 1953) (New York: 1954), p. 754.

[69] *The New York Times,* October 9, 1949, part IV, p. 12.

[70] *Facts on File Year Book 1953,* Vol. 13, No. 672 (September 11-17, 1953), p. 305 g².

[71] See Benjamin Azkin, *New States and International Organizations* (Paris: UNESCO, 1955), p. 20. He found that an "old state" like Thailand was less active than many new states because of a lack of aspiration for such a role on the part of Thailand. He also observed: "Though Afghanistan is an older state, it has developed less trained personnel and is less active on the international level than are the younger states of Isreal, Pakistan or the Philippines." *Ibid.*

[72] *The Times* London, July 20, 1964, p. 11.

world's limelight."[73] The effect of this introversion was recognized by India's Foreign Minister when he indicated that "his country's voice had diminished in international affairs."[74] India's participation at the 1964 Cairo Conference of non-aligned states was the antithesis of active participation. It was observed that "at the non-aligned conference in Cairo next month Shastri will be an interested participant but he will also—to borrow the Japanese phrase—be adopting a low posture."[75] Under Mrs. Indhira Gandhi's leadership, the Indians seem to think of themselves as "the leaders of the neutralist world."[76] India's willingness in convening an "unaligned parley" of the heads of governments of India, Egypt and Yugoslavia[77] seemed to suggest a swing towards a more activist policy than the one pursued by Mr. Shastri.

INDIA'S UTILIZATION OF THE UNITED NATIONS
TO ACHIEVE HER OBJECTIVES

India's active participation in the councils of the United Nations stemmed from her desire to invoke the world body in the furtherance of her foreign policy objectives. Mr. Nehru summed up the foreign policy objectives of India in an address at Columbia University in 1949. They included the pursuit of peace through non-alignment, the liberation of subject peoples, the maintenance of freedom, the elimination of racial discrimination and the elimination of want, disease, and ignorance.[78] Mr. Swaran Singh, India's Foreign Min-

---

[73] *Ibid.*

[74] *The New York Times,* December 3, 1964, p. 18.

[75] *The Times,* London, September 9, 1964, p. 13. Mr. Shastri was more a reluctant participant than an interested participant. India was cool toward the proposed 1965 Afro-Asian Conference that was never held.

[76] *Ibid.* November 20, 1965, p. 9.

[77] *The New York Times,* May 6, 1966, p. 8.

[78] Nehru, *Visit to America, op. cit.,* pp. 29-30. See also Gupta, *op. cit.,* p. 1.

ister, reiterated in 1964 these objectives as the basic principles of Indian foreign policy.[79] Madame Pandit made it
clear that India would fully utilize the United Nations in the
achievement of India's objective of world peace. She said
that "India is an active member of the United Nations and
willingly offers her service when it is needed to ease tension
and promote good will. . . . Her chosen role demands that
she exert herself in whatever capacity offers itself in the
interests of peace."[80] India's delegates at the United Nations
believed that only through a vigorous and determined effort
could peace be maintained. To pursue any other course
would be to suppress India's individuality and therefore "to
reduce its capacity to play an active role in safeguarding
peace."[81] Sir B. N. Rau explained India's role at the United
Nations by saying that "one country, with faith and determination, can win through in time. It is in this hope that we

[79] *Lok Sabha Debates,* Third Series, vol. XXXIV, No. 15, Ninth Session (September 25, 1964) (New Delhi: Lok Sabha Secretariat, 1964),
column 3780. Appadorai noted the same objectives, see Azkin, *op. cit.,* p.
52. Kundra added some more objectives to those stated by Nehru and
scaled them as follows: "non-involvement in a Third World-War," development of Indian economy, winning of international support on Kashmir,
integration of foreign pockets on India's coasts, securing a fair treatment
and dignity for Indians settled abroad, cooperation with neighbors, see
Kundra, *op. cit.,* p. 59. Mr. Swaran Singh emphasized the latter two objectives in 1964. See *The New York Times,* December 3, 1964, p. 18. See
Norman D. Palmer, *The Indian Political System, op. cit.,* p. 243; and K.
P. Karunakaran, *India in World Affairs 1947-50* (London: Oxford University Press, 1952), pp. 23-47. Eldridge summarized the objectives of
India's foreign policy as follows: an active role in promoting peace and
disarmament, strong support for the United Nations, emphasis on the
peaceful settlement of disputes, anti-colonialism and anti-racialism,
and a code of international behavior based on Panch Shila, see P. J. Eldridge, "India's Non-Alignment Policy Reviewed," *Australian Outlook,*
Vol. 19, No. 2 (August 1965), p. 146.

[80] Pandit, *op. cit.,* p. 435. She explained that India stood for peace and
would devote all her resources and energy toward the abolition of all
causes which would lead to war. See C. Kondapi "Indian Opinion of the
United Nations," *International Organization,* Vol. 5 (November 1951),
p. 712.

[81] Rau, "India and World Peace," *op. cit.,* pp. 631-632.

who have the honor to represent India in the United Nations are trying to carry out our duties."[82] Mr. G. L. Mehta stressed that peace could be strengthened by making use of the international bodies through active participation. He observed that "the way to avoid wars now is not to be aloof and isolated but to participate in international bodies and seek to strengthen the forces of peace. That is what India with its limited resources and despite its domestic obligations wants to do."[83] A study on India's role in the United Nations recognized India's utilization of the organization in the pursuit of her foreign policy goals. According to Berkes and Bedi, "India's behavior in the United Nations has been particularly marked by a tendency to invoke the organization as an instrument for the advancement of certain causes, most of which it has insistently brought forward in terms of highly moral considerations."[84]

India found the United Nations useful in the achievement of her foreign policy goals such as the freeing of dependent peoples.[85] The United Nations provided India ample opportunities for implementing her objectives. The extent of Indian support for the UN depended upon the degree of usefulness of the United Nations for India. The satisfaction in bringing independence to dependent peoples by invoking the organization year after year deepened India's dedication to the United Nations. According to Fontera, "India's view that the General Assembly is the final judge of whether or not a colonial area has attained complete independence and her attempts to widen the scope of the Assembly's Com-

[82] Sir Benegal Narsing Rau, "What Asia Can Give the World," *Vital Speeches*, Vol. 17, No. 15 (May 15, 1951), p. 470.

[83] G. L. Mehta, "India in World Affairs," *Vital Speeches*, Vol. 21, No. 18 (July 1, 1955), p. 1323.

[84] Ross N. Berkes and Mohinder S. Bedi, *The Diplomacy of India: India's Foreign Policy in the United Nations* (Stanford: Stanford University Press, 1958), p. 44.

[85] See the chapter on India's anti-colonial policy at the United Nations.

mittee on Information from non-self-governing territories is a reflection of her faith in the United Nations—especially the General Assembly."[86] India's successful use of the United Nations in the pursuit of her objectives demonstrated her dependence on the world body.

Berkes and Bedi pointed out that "India's dependence on the United Nations implies a stake in developing its effectiveness."[87] Fervently appealing for loyalty to the United Nations, Mr. M. C. Chagla said that "if we want the United Nations to become a living organization, it is not sufficient to sign charters or pass solemn resolutions, we must conform loyally and honestly to the principles we have subscribed to in the Charter."[88] According to Madame Pandit the important thing was that "we should all observe faithfully the spirit and letter of the Charter, its principles and procedures, not only when it is convenient to us, not only when it helps us to pursue aims and policies which may have no connection with the Charter, but at all times and in relation to all problems and difficulties."[89] Mr. Nehru stressed that the United Nations "should be encouraged and supported in every way, and should be allowed to develop into some kind of world government or world order."[90] However, Indian leaders seemed to have been dismayed over the attitude that the Security Council adopted on Kashmir.[91] Nevertheless,

[86] Richard M. Fontera, "Anti-Colonialism as a Basic Indian Foreign Policy," *Western Political Quarterly,* Vol. 13 (June 1960), p. 431.

[87] Berkes and Bedi, *op. cit.,* p. 2. According to them, India had a "consuming dedication" for the United Nations and the latter was "an incomparable vehicle of policy" for the former, *Ibid,* p. 203.

[88] "Resolutions adopted at plenary meetings," *United Nations Weekly Bulletin,* Vol. 1, No. 18 (December 3, 1946), p. 5.

[89] United Nations, General Assembly, Second Session, *Official Records,* Vol. 1, 85th plenary meeting (17 September 1947) (Lake Success, 1948), p. 137.

[90] Nehru, *India's Foreign Policy, op. cit.,* p. 33.

[91] Finding support over Kashmir was one of several objectives of India, and it should be noted the UN was useful for India in the implementation of the other objectives.

the difficulties India incurred over Kashmir did not diminish India's support of the United Nations either significantly or permanently. When some Indian parliamentarians expressed their disappointment in 1952 at the way the United Nations was handling the Kashmir issue, Mr. Nehru lectured them saying that the United Nations, in spite of its many faults, was "a basic and fundamental thing in the structure of the world today. Not to have it or to do away with it would be a tragedy for the world. Therefore, I do not wish this country of ours to do anything which weakens the gradual development of some kind of a world structure."[92]

Addressing the United Nations General Assembly in 1948 Mr. Nehru pledged that "we adhere completely to the principles and purposes of the United Nations Charter and that we shall try, to the best of our ability, to work for the realization of those principles and purposes."[93] Replying to criticism of the United Nations in India, Mr. Nehru rallied to its support by warning that if "the UNO ceased to function today, it would be a disaster for the world. . . . It would be a wrong thing for any country, in a fit of impatience, to sever its relations with this body and weaken it in the process."[94]

The same trend of thought continued in the attitude of Indian leaders toward the United Nations in recent years. Mr. Swaran Singh, Nehru's successor at the Indian Foreign Office, appealed to Indonesia not to withdraw from the United Nations and not to do anything that would weaken the United Nations. He also "appealed to all countries to

[92] Nehru, *Jawaharlal Nehru's Speeches 1949-1953, op. cit.,* p. 349. India's Congress party expressed that "India would continue to support the United Nations" in the hope that some day it would become an effective instrument for forging peace. See *The New York Times,* September 15, 1952, p. 1.

[93] Nehru, *Independence and After, op. cit.,* p. 323. See also Karunakaran, *India in World Affairs, 1947-50, op. cit.,* p. 247.

[94] Nehru, *Jawaharlal Nehru's Speeches 1949-1953, op. cit.,* p. 199.

persuade Indonesia not to quit the United Nations. By walking out of the United Nations, Indonesia had given a jolt to the world body, Mr. Swaran Singh said. Whatever Indonesia's complaints might be, she should not do anything that would weaken the UN on which rested the future hopes of humanity."[95] Prime Minister Shastri expressed India's deep interest "in preserving the United Nations and further strengthening it" as much as she could.[96] Mr. Shastri said that India was a staunch supporter of the United Nations and he reaffirmed India's "unflinching support for the United Nations."[97]

President Radhakrishnan expressed India's steadfast support for the United Nations by stating that "India had extreme faith in the organization and would do everything in its power to strengthen the authority and influence of the United Nations."[98] He referred to India's contribution to the United Nations in Korea, Gaza and the Congo and pointed out that India's "faith in the United Nations is illustrated by our work in the United Nations and its agencies, on the several commissions and committees."[99] He mentioned the assistance that the United Nations provided in finding solutions to the West Irian, the Arab-Israeli, the Cyprus and the

[95] *India News,* January 15, 1965, p. 1.

[96] *The Hindu Weekly Review,* November 8, 1965, p. 3. Premier Shastri and the Prime Minister of Afghanistan reiterated "their firm support for the United Nations and stressed that all efforts should be made to build up the strength and prestige of the world organization." See *India News,* March 5, 1965, p. 2. At the 1964 Cairo Conference of the Non-Aligned nations, Mr. Shastri said that they should support the UN "not merely in words but in action." See *India News,* January 21, 1966, p. 5.

[97] Lal Bahadur Shastri, *Speeches of Prime Minister Lal Bahadur Shastri* (New Delhi Publications Division, Ministry of Information and Broadcasting, Government of India, 1965) pp. 6, 104, 106.

[98] President of India sees United Nations Giving Conscience to World Community, *United Nations Review,* Vol. 10, No. 7 (July 1963), p. 51.

[99] India News, November 5, 1965, p. 6. Madame Pandit said that she could never have accepted the presidency of the General Assembly if she had not had the "fullest confidence" in the United Nations' worth and "faith in its future."

Kashmir problems.[100] Although the United Nations did not do all that could be expected of it in solving these problems, Mr. Radhakrishnan emphasized that it had not done unsubstantial work and that we should look to the work it did in the Congo, "the encouragement it gave to liberation movements and the way it brought about a dispassionate and objective discussion of the problems of disarmament and a nuclear test ban."[101] This steadfast support stemmed from the satisfaction that India derived from the United Nations in the pursuit of her foreign policy objectives.

INDIA'S CONCEPTION OF A STRONG UNITED NATIONS

A strong United Nations meant quite a different thing to India than to the proponents of the "Acheson Plan"[102] or to the advocates of "supranational organization."[103] India viewed that the United Nations should be a universal organization, not greatly dominated by either of the two blocs, reflecting the world as it was and serving the purposes of the Charter through the cooperative effort of its members. According to Mr. Nehru "the whole concept of the United Nations when it started was to take the world as it was, with its conflicts and its differences and help to bring it together."[104] As earlier noted India also considered the United

[100] *Ibid.*

[101] "President of India sees United Nations Giving Conscience to World Community," *op. cit.*, p. 51. Mr. Nehru recognized United Nations service in the cause of peace and in the liberation of subject peoples and hoped that the United Nations would "advance from strength to strength" in furthering these objectives. See "Two presidents, A Prime Minister Address General Assembly," *United Nations Review*, Vol. 8, No. 12 (December, 1961), p. 138. See also Karunakaran, *India in World Affairs 1950-53, op. cit.*, p. 147.

[102] Karunakaran, *India in World Affairs 1950-53, op. cit.*, p. 138.

[103] Berkes and Bedi, *op. cit.*, p. 2.

[104] Nehru, *India's Foreign Policy, op. cit.*, p. 181. See Norman Cousins "Conversations with Nehru, part I," *Saturday Review of Literature*, Vol. XXXIV, No. 15, (April 14, 1951), p. 19.

Nations as a world forum of sovereign states that met together to tackle world problems in order to find peaceful
solutions.[105] Mr. Nehru thought that "when people met and
discussed things, they would not go to war and some way out
would be found."[106] Emphasizing the cooperative character
of the United Nations Mr. Nehru said that "there can be no
doubt that the mere fact of its existence has saved us from
many dangers and conflicts."[107] Mr. A. R. Mudaliar liked to
describe the meetings of the United Nations as "the safety
valve through which the pent-up passions of statesmen are
released without detriment to world peace."[108]

India's conception of the United Nations facilitated her
desire for active participation in world affairs by providing
excellent opportunities for influencing policy in matters
which came within the purview of the United Nations and
most international crises were likely to do so.[109] India
claimed to be a spokesman of the Afro-Asians, the non-
aligned, the under-developed and the small states and used
the United Nations and its councils in pursuing such a role.
It was observed that "the nature of India's policy makes it
essential that she should cultivate diplomacy by conference.
The meetings of the Commonwealth and the assemblies of

[105] See M. Y. Kamath "India at the United Nations," *United Asia,* Vol.
9 (September 1957), p. 229.
[106] S. N. Varma, "India's Policy in the United Nations with respect to
the maintenance of International Peace and Security," p. 91. Citing *Special
Press Release* (Washington, D.C.: Government of India Information
Services, n.d.), p. 3. See Alan de Russet, "An Understanding of Indian
Foreign Policy," *International Relations,* Vol. 1, No. 11 (April 1959), p.
551. See also Kamath, *op. cit.,* p. 229.
[107] Nehru, *India's Foreign Policy, op. cit.,* p. 167. To Krishna Menon
the United Nations was "a center for harmonizing different views and for
the relaxation of tensions." See United Nations, General Assembly, Thirteenth Session, *Official Records,* 792nd plenary meeting, agenda item 3
(13 December 1958) (New York, 1958), p. 612.
[108] Mudaliar, *op. cit.,* p. 400.
[109] Falls, *op. cit.,* p. 598. See also Nair, "Non-Alignment, History, Ideology, Prospects," *op. cit.,* pp. 60-61.

the United Nations are of greater significance to her than to most other members."[110] India found in the world body an organization in which it was able to realize its equality and a means for maximizing its influence in world affairs.[111]

India suggested proposals to make the United Nations effective as an instrument of peace. In 1960, Mr. Menon suggested that the General Assembly and other United Nations bodies, instead of passing draft resolutions put forward by one side or another, "should definitely give directives." He insisted that "the Assembly had to take greater responsibility."[112] Thus India never visualized the United Nations in terms of a mere "debating body."[113] On the contrary, Mr. Nehru pointed out in 1960 that "people everywhere looked to this Assembly to take some step to ease the situation and to lessen world tension."[114]

India's delegates at the United Nations endorsed the United Nations military presence in the Congo and attempted to enlarge the scope of the organization's activity in the Congo. Mr. Krishna Menon contended that "the United Nations projected itself by military might. It did not send an invading army, but force was required."[115] He demanded that the United Nations should either "govern or get out" without concealing his preference for the former. He urged strong action by the United Nations and pointed out that the Organization was not weak and as a result of

[110] "India's Foreign Policy," *The Fortnightly*, Vol. 182 (July 1954), p. 11.
[111] Nair, "Non-Alignment in World Affairs," *op. cit.*, p. 31.
[112] "Summary of the General Debate-Part 11," *United Nations Review*, Vol. 7, No. 6 (December 1960), p. 81.
[113] Nehru, *India's Foreign Policy, op. cit.*, p. 181.
[114] "Summary of the General Debate," *United Nations Review*, Vol. 7, No. 5 (November 1960), p. 82.
[115] "Assembly Debate on the Congo," *United Nations Review*, Vol. 8, No. 2 (February 1961), p. 7.

new admissions had become even stronger. He set aside his favorite theme of national sovereignty and stated that "here we are not trampling down on the sovereignty of a country, we are protecting the authority of the United Nations Charter."[116] Mr. Nehru felt that it was of the utmost importance that the work the United Nations had undertaken in the Congo should succeed and should yield results.[117] He also urged the United Nations to take vigorous and strong action in the Congo. When some Indian parliamentarians criticized the United Nations passive role in the Congo and demanded the withdrawal of Indian forces from the Congo, Mr. Nehru utilized the occasion to urge the United Nations to take stronger action in the Congo. He warned that "we have put up with many difficulties that face us, but I cannot, if our people are not treated properly and given opportunities to do the work for which they were sent, guarantee that the question will not arise whether it is worthwhile keeping them there or not."[118] Mr. Nehru favored the use of force to achieve the United Nations objectives when he said that the United Nations authority in the Congo "should function even if it is necessary to use armed force and not merely look on while others use armed force for a wrong purpose."[119]

The United Nations request for Indian combat troops provided India with an opportunity to influence United

[116] United Nations, General Assembly, Fifteenth Session, *Official Records,* part I, Vol. 2, 950th plenary meeting, agenda item 85 (16 December 1960) (New York, 1961), p. 1319.

[117] United Nations, General Assembly, Sixteenth Session, *Official Records,* Vol. II, 1051st plenary meeting (10 November 1961) (New York, 1962), p. 621. See Nehru, *India's Foreign Policy, op. cit.,* p. 523. He said that the failure of United Nations in Congo would "make it difficult for it to function in the future in any like emergency." See also *The New York Times,* January 7, 1962, p. 25.

[118] Nehru, *India's Foreign Policy, op. cit.,* p. 519.

[119] *Ibid.,* p. 526.

Nations policy in the Congo. On receiving the request for combat troops, India informed the Secretary-General that "we had not approved of the way in which the United Nations has been functioning in the Congo. We had no desire, therefore, to send our armed forces to the Congo unless the policy of the United Nations changed and was brought more in line with our views on the subject."[120] The reply of the Secretary-General was obviously satisfactory to India for India decided to contribute combat forces. According to Palmer "the dispatch of Indian troops to join the United Nations forces in the Congo, at a critical time, was a major contribution to the efforts of the UN in that troubled area, and represented a major policy decision of India."[121] It could also be said that India influenced the United Nations to pursue a policy more in line with India's views. In the case of the Congo, India desired an effective and a stronger role for the United Nations and her support reached its full capacity when the United Nations policy, to borrow Nehru's phrase, was brought more in line with India's views.

The United Nations espoused and served the causes of peace, promotion of friendly relations, freedom of dependent peoples, disarmament and economic development. These ideals were cherished by India. To serve these purposes further the Indians desired that the United Nations "should develop into a truly international organization of world-wide prestige"[122] and "should develop into some kind of a world order or world government."[123] Indian objectives happened to be consistent with the objectives of the United

[120] *Ibid.* The strength of Indian forces steadily increased up to 10,000 and India provided jet aircraft, although India badly needed the sparse aircraft for its own defense purposes. See *The Times,* London, October 2, 1961, p. 9.

[121] Norman D. Palmer, "India's Foreign Policy," *Political Quarterly,* Vol. 33, No. 4 (October-December 1962), p. 392.

[122] Karunakaran, *India in World Affairs 1950-53, op. cit.,* p. 149.

[123] Murti, *op. cit.,* p. 77.

Nations.[124] India, logically, became a staunch supporter of the United Nations and a standard-bearer of the movement for a stronger and effective United Nations to serve the purposes of the charter through the cooperative efforts of its members. One might agree with Palmer's observation that "India is interested in promoting the work of the United Nations which it regards as consistent with its own national interest, and in blocking any actions or resolutions which it regards as detrimental to its national interest. Fortunately India feels, as do other neutral states, that the area of mutual interest is a very wide one."[125]

[124] A study of the Council of World Affairs, India, concluded that the objectives of India and those of the United Nations, generally, "do not clash." See I.C.W.A. Study, *op. cit.*, p. 206. With the exception of Kashmir, no major conflict seemed to exist between India and the world body.

[125] Palmer, "The Afro-Asians in the United Nations," *op. cit.*, p. 160.

2

Policy Toward Amending
the United Nations Charter

India opposed Western attempts to amend the United
Nations Charter in the belief that they would increase the
imbalance in the United Nations in favor of the West.
India's emphasis on the cooperative character of the United
Nations and her stress on the need for unanimity among the
great powers prompted her to resist several proposals to
amend the Charter.

RESISTANCE TO THE REMOVAL OF THE VETO

India consistently maintained that the veto should be
retained. In 1946, Mrs. Vijaya Lakshmi Pandit said: "I
would myself prefer to look upon the so-called veto in a

positive way and as the necessary device for securing that vital decision by the great powers rest on unanimity and not on disregard of the total opposition to any proposal by one of them."[1] During the First Session of the General Assembly, Mr. V. K. Krishna Menon maintained that the solution for the regulation of the use of the veto laid with the permanent members of the Security Council. He stated that "his delegation could not support any resolution which could not commend itself to the major elements in the General Assembly. Any resolution concerning the 'veto' which was not acceptable to all members vitally concerned would not be of any practical value at the present time."[2] Prime Minister Jawharlal Nehru contended that the unanimity rule recognized the reality of the moment and pointed out that the removal of the veto could only come about by some kind of general agreement and that if that veto was removed by a vote or decision of the United Nations, there was little doubt that the United Nations would cease to be that very instant."[3] Acknowledging the Brazilian observation that the work of the United Nations at San Francisco would not have been possible if it had not been for the agreement over the veto, Mr. Menon insisted "that the continuance of the United Nations required the veto."[4]

While pleading for moderation and restraint in the exercise of the veto, the Indian delegation emphasized that "the

[1] United Nations, General Assembly, First Session, Second Part, *Official Records,* 37th plenary meeting (25 October 1946) (Lake Success, 1947), p. 733.
[2] United Nations, General Assembly, First Session, Second Part, *Official Records,* First Committee, 42nd meeting (8 December 1946) (Lake Success, 1946), p. 286. See also I.C.W.A. Study, *op. cit.,* p. 42; "The United Nations: A Symposium on its ogranization and future," *Seminar* (March, 1962), p. 13.
[3] Nehru, *India's Foreign Policy, op. cit.,* p. 33.
[4] United Nations, General Assembly, Ninth Session, *Official Records,* 492nd plenary meeting, agenda item 9 (6 October 1954) (Lake Success, 1955), p. 232.

permanent members of the (Security) Council have an obligation to strive to the utmost to widen the area of agreement among its members."[5] Indian delegate Mr. B. Shiva Rao thought that "the only practical method to ensure the normal functioning of the Security Council was to remove the existing differences between the five permanent members."[6] He made it clear that India was opposed to the immediate and complete abolition of the right of veto. Indians looked at the veto as a necessary provision which prevented the domination and the use of the Security Council by a bloc of powers to implement their policies.[7] Some Indians felt that the Soviet use of the veto was of value to a small state over disputes in which the Western powers took a partisan stand. Mr. Arthur S. Lall pointed out that the Soviets used their veto power in their interest and also "in defense of the interests of other states, generally Asian or African states, when it has appeared that the other party to the dispute or situation before the Security Council could count on the support of other great powers in the Council."[8] India's belief in the existence of an imbalance in the Security Council and her desire to minimize great power confrontation led her to resist the removal of the veto. India feared that the removal of the veto without the consent of the Soviet Union would lead to the latter's withdrawal from the United Nations and thus would affect the universal character of the international organization.

[5] United Nations, General Assembly, Second Session, *Official Records,* Vol. 1, 85th plenary meeting (19 September 1947) (New York, 1948), p. 135.

[6] United Nations, General Assembly, Third Session, Part I, *Official Records,* Ad Hoc Political Committee, 19th meeting (30 November 1948) (Paris, 1949), p. 223.

[7] Karunakaran, *India in World Affairs 1950-53, op. cit.,* p. 148.

[8] Arthur S. Lall, "The Asian Nations and the United Nations," *International Organization,* Vol. XIX, No. 3 (Summer 1965), p. 734. For the expression of a similar view see "Off White Elephant," *The Economist,* Vol. 202 (February 10, 1962), p. 495.

INDIA'S ATTITUDE TOWARD THE INTERIM COMMITTEE

In 1947 Mr. M. C. Setalvad, a member of the Indian delegation stated that the Indian delegation agreed, in principle, to the establishment of an "Interim Committee" of the General Assembly "purely as an experimental measure." According to him the objective of the committee was "the coordination and integration of the responsibilities of the Assembly and the Security Council."[9] Both Mr. Shiva Rao and Mr. Setalvad thought that the Interim Committee had done much useful work. However, they indicated their reluctance to support any proposal to continue the Interim Committee indefinitely. Mr. Setalvad pointed out that there was strong opposition to the Interim Committee and some members refused to take part in it. He thought that the cooperation of the Communist states was essential and wondered that "if it would not be preferable to replace the Interim Committee by one or several *ad hoc* committees among which the General Assembly could distribute the work."[10]

[9] United Nations, General Assembly, Second Session, *Official Records,* First Committee 76th meeting (16 October 1947) (New York, 1948) p. 151. In 1948 Mr. Setalvad reiterated that India would support the continuation of the Interim Committee for another year "as an experimental measure." See United Nations, General Assembly, Third Session, Part I, *Official Records,* Ad Hoc Political Committee, 2nd meeting (17 November 1948) (Paris, 1949), p. 15. In India's view the Interim Committee was a subsidiary body of the Assembly and would not usurp the powers of the Security Council. See United Nations, General Assembly, Second Session, *Official Records,* First Committee, 95th meeting (5 November 1947) (New York, 1947), pp. 317-318. India insisted that matters of substance could only be decided by the Assembly and not by the Interim Committee. See United Nations, General Assembly, Fifth Session, *Official Records,* Ad Hoc Political Committee, 60th meeting (28 November 1950) (Lake Success, 1951), p. 386.

[10] United Nations, General Assembly, Third Session, Part I, *Official Records,* Ad Hoc Political Committee, 2nd meeting (17 November 1948) (Paris, 1949), p. 14.

INDIA'S REACTION TO THE ACHESON PLAN

India expressed serious misgivings at the United States' attempts to employ the United Nations to achieve American foreign policy objectives in Korea. India raised strong objections to Section C of the Uniting for Peace Resolution which referred to the maintenance of national units for service under the United Nations upon requisition by the Security Council or the General Assembly. Sir B. N. Rau stated that in the consideration of his government, that was not the time for stressing the military aspect of the United Nations. He felt that the delegates "should rather concentrate on improving the machinery of the United Nations for the tasks of peace."[11] Mr. A. C. N. Nambiar argued that "at a time when all peoples of the world desired peace, that part of the resolution gave the impression that the United Nations was more concerned with perfecting its endorsement machinery than with promoting international cooperation and mutual goodwill."[12] It was believed by some Indians that the Uniting for Peace Resolution would make a great change in the purpose and working of the United Nations by making a majority decision the basis of its functioning, while Big Five unanimity was the "legal and moral foundation of the United Nations." Mr. C. Kondapi thought that the Acheson Plan would weaken the United Nations and would strengthen the Anglo-American bloc. He argued that "the United Nations' military powers were not meant to be used

[11] United Nations, General Assembly, Fifth Session, *Official Records,* Vol. 1, 301st plenary meeting (2 November 1950) (New York, 1951), p. 336. Mr. Rau said that the Security Council was functioning like a war council. India abstained on the Uniting for Peace Resolution.

[12] United Nations, General Assembly, Fifth Session, *Official Records,* First Committee, 369th meeting (19 October 1950) (New York, 1951), p. 161.

unless the five permanent members of the Security Council were agreed. The Acheson Plan pushed through the United Nations by the Anglo-American majority bloc converts the United Nations into a weapon against the rival Soviet bloc."[13] India feared that such action would lead to the disruption of the United Nations.

THE CHARTER AND THE ADMISSION OF NEW MEMBERS

India insisted that the Charter provisions should be strictly adhered to in admitting members into the United Nations. Mr. Setalvad stated that the admission of new members must be subject to the concurrent vote of the five permanent members of the Security Council and any solution to the problem of admission of members should come about by an agreement among the five great powers.[14] In the absence of the principle of universality India desired the retention of the veto over admissions because she feared that the absence of the veto over admissions would increase the imbalance in the United Nations in favor of the West. India felt that the veto was necessary to prevent the packing of the United Nations, with friends, by a majority decision of the Security Council.[15] Madame Pandit recognized that "the attitude of certain members of the (Security) Council merely demonstrated the existence of blocs within the United Nations. If delegations were reluctant to admit new members,

[13] C. Kondapi, "Indian Opinion of the United Nations," *International Organization,* Vol. 5 (November 1951), p. 721. According to Kondapi, Indian public opinion believed that the Acheson Plan was a part of "the Anglo-American jockeying to by-pass and dominate the United Nations." *Ibid.* For the expression of a similar view see Karunakaran, *India in World Affairs 1950-53, op cit.,* pp. 136, 138.

[14] United Nations, General Assembly, Third Session, Part I, *Official Records,* Ad Hoc Political Committee, 9th meeting (23 November 1948) (Paris, 1949), p. 90.

[15] I.C.W.A. Study, *op. cit.,* p. 56.

it was because they did not wish to strengthen opposing groups."[16] When a proposal was made to ask the International Court of Justice whether the Security Council could recommend the admission of a state without the affirmative vote of all its permanent members, Mr. Menon remarked that the General Assembly "would be overriding the accepted practice of the Council and deliberately passing over its competence. And such usurpation of powers, such disregard of an established jurisdiction, might subsequently be extended to other spheres."[17]

Considering the report of the Special Committee on Admission of new members, Mr. Menon charged that "instead of a family of nations the United Nations was being made an exclusive club in which one group was trying to exclude the candidates of another group and thus to maintain an Assembly of like-minded members."[18] He argued that "it was never the idea of the founders of the United Nations or the governments which participated that we should, in any form, become an exclusive club or a holy alliance."[19] He stated that the problem of admissions "could not be solved by some sort of mandatory decision, even

[16] United Nations, General Assembly, Second Session, *Official Records, First Committee*, 101st meeting (18 November 1947) (Lake Success, 1948), p. 364.
[17] United Nations, General Assembly, Seventh Session, *Official Records, Ad Hoc Political Committee*, 47th meeting, item 19 (17 December 1952) (New York, 1953), p. 294. Mr. Menon held that the question of admissions was a political matter and it was for the Security Council to decide whether the issue was a substantive or a procedural one. He opposed, unsuccessfully, the establishment of a Special Committee to consider the issue of admissions for it would lead to the pressuring of the Security Council. In his view the committee could not yield the desired results, *Ibid.*
[18] United Nations, General Assembly, Eighth Session, *Official Records, Ad Hoc Political Committee*, 12th meeting (15 October 1953) (New York, 1954), p. 59.
[19] United Nations, General Assembly, Tenth Session, *Official Records*, 533rd plenary meeting (4 October 1955) (New York, 1956), p. 234.

though it might be taken by a two-thirds majority. It was a matter for negotiation."[20] It was his view that a solution to the problem of admissions could not be expected through a revision of the Charter. According to Mr. Menon the General Assembly could remind the Security Council of its functions and responsibilities and of world public opinion but the Assembly could not force the Council to act nor could it dictate terms under which the Council should take steps.[21]

A CAUTIOUS STAND ON CHARTER REVISION

Mr. C. C. Shah, a member of the Indian delegation to the United Nations, conceded that the Charter was not perfect and considered that the problem of revising the Charter was both a legal and a political one. He cautioned that "any revision would have to be realistic, not utopian, designed to make it a more effective instrument and strengthen the organization."[22] He did not think that a discussion of possible Charter revision would increase tension in the world but he felt that it was necessary to exercise restraint in debate. During the Tenth Session Mr. Menon indicated that India was willing to consider such "alterations" as are made in all written constitutions, but was not prepared to entertain any

[20] United Nations, General Assembly, Eighth Session, *Official Records,* Ad Hoc Political Committee, 12th meeting (15 October 1953) (New York, 1954), p. 61.

[21] United Nations, General Assembly, Ninth Session, *Official Records,* Ad Hoc Political Committee, 25th meeting, agenda item 21 (11 November 1954) (New York, 1955), p. 109. See also United Nations, General Assembly, Tenth Session, *Official Records,* Ad Hoc Political Committee, 32nd meeting, agenda item 21 (7 December 1955) (New York, 1956), p. 152.

[22] United Nations, General Assembly, Eighth Session, *Official Records,* Sixth Committee, 363rd meeting, item 54 (1 October 1953) (New York, 1954), p. 78.

proposal to convene a conference like the San Francisco Conference or to make fundamental changes in the Charter. He explained that India would "support any move that does not seek to throw out the baby with the bath water, that does not seek to raise unnecessary controversy, that does not add more difficulty to the many difficulties which we have to solve. We have no objection to subscribing to any move that arises as a matter of general agreement and compromise, but my government is definitely opposed to the establishment of any elaborate machinery or to the taking of any overt step which demands from us a full-scale review of the Charter."[23] He stated that India would agree to place the subject of charter review on the agenda of the Assembly and, for the sake of compromise, would support a study of it.[24] Mr. Menon contended that it was not the Charter that was wrong, "it is we ourselves, and therefore we could very well devote our endeavors in the coming year to improving our loyalties in regard to the spirit and purposes of the Charter."[25]

He unsuccessfully opposed a proposal to convene a general conference to review the Charter "at an appropriate

[23] United Nations, General Assembly, Tenth Session, *Official Records,* 533rd plenary meeting, agenda item 9 (4 October 1955) (New York, 1956), p. 234.

[24] United Nations, General Assembly, Tenth Session, *Official Records,* 543rd plenary meeting, agenda item 55 (17 November 1955) (New York, 1956), p. 320.

[25] United Nations, General Assembly, Tenth Session, *Official Records,* 533rd plenary meeting, agenda item 9 (4 October 1955) (New York, 1956,) p. 234. Madame Pandit expressed the same view. See *The New York Times,* November 16, 1953, p. 2. A similar view was held by Lakshmi N. Menon. See K. B. Rai, "India's Attitude Towards the Revision of the United Nations Charter-II," *Foreign Affairs Reports* (India), Vol. 14 (June 1965), p. 83. See also Berkes and Bedi, *op. cit.,* p. 4. To Menon, problems of disarmament and economic development were more important than the problem of charter revision. Mr. Nehru gave priority to the problems of the Congo and disarmament over reorganization of the U.N. Secretariat, See *The Times,* London, February 28, 1961, p. 9.

time." He felt that such a proposal would throw into the hands of "snatch majorities" the determination of the appropriate time for revising the Charter. The Indian belief in the existence of an imbalance in the United Nations was expressed by Mr. Menon by saying that "our experience in this Assembly is that the majority has a tendency to slide in one direction."[26] It was this feeling of the domination of the General Assembly by a bloc of powers that prompted Mr. Menon to mention the dangers in allowing the Assembly to exercise security functions during the Suez Crisis when the Assembly exercised considerable powers. He said that "we must carefully warn ourselves that the security functions of the United Nations do not willy-nilly and forever shift to the Assembly. There are dangers inherent in this, and it is for us to consider them carefully."[27]

In 1959, Mr. C. S. Jha of the Indian delegation cautioned the General Assembly against taking any hasty steps over the issue of amending the United Nations Charter. He said that India did not favor "the setting up of a committee to study the possibilities of arriving at an agreement regarding the amendment of the Charter. We do not think that this will produce very good results. It may be taken, on the contrary, as some kind of pressure on one of the big powers which, for reasons of its own which it is quite entitled to hold, is not prepared to accept an amendment without

[26] United Nations, General Assembly, Tenth Session, *Official Records,* 543rd plenary meeting, agenda item 55 (17 November 1955) (New York, 1956), p. 321. This observation was made before sixteen states joined the United Nations through a "package deal." After these admissions Mr. Menon remarked that they "now have additional strength in the United Nations" and he noted that the imbalance of Asian representation in the General Assembly was rectified to "certain extent." See United Nations, General Assembly, Tenth Session, *Official Records,* 556th plenary meeting (15 December 1955) (New York, 1956), p. 454.

[27] United Nations, General Assembly, Eleventh Session, *Official Records,* Vol. I, 611th plenary meeting, agenda item 9 (6 December 1956) (New York, 1957), p. 576.

certain conditions being fulfilled."[28] Mr. Nehru stressed the need for an understanding among the permanent members of the Security Council on the issue of Charter revision. He stated that India, in spite of her desire for a change in the structure of the United Nations, wished "to proceed slowly and with agreement and not to press any change which would involve an immediate amendment of the Charter and the raising of heated controversies."[29] Reiterating India's emphasis on a certain measure of unanimity among the great powers on Charter amendment, Mr. Nehru observed that India did not press for changes in the Charter because "one thing necessary for some measure of unanimity is the cooling down of the hot war or rather the cold war toning down."[30] It was feared in India that the attempts to make radical changes in the Charter, without the consent of all the great powers, would increase tension.[31]

Mr. Krishna Menon opposed the idea of the General Assembly adopting a resolution, with a two-thirds majority, recommending the expansion of the membership of the Security Council and the Economic and Social Council and then submitting it for ratification by governments. He criti-

[28] United Nations, General Assembly, Fourteenth Session, *Official Records,* 843rd plenary meeting, agenda items 19, 20 and 21 (25 November 1959) (New York, 1960), p. 607. See also United Nations, General Assembly, Fourteenth Session, *Official Records,* Special Political Committee, 130th meeting, agenda items 19, 20 and 21 (15 October 1959) (New York, 1960), p. 14.

[29] Nehru, *India's Foreign Policy, op. cit.,* p. 218. See also "Summary of General Debate," *United Nations Review,* Vol. 7, No. 5 (November 1960), p. 82. The same view was expressed by Mr. Menon when he said that India "has been a consistent opponent of any amendment of the Charter without getting agreement among the great powers, because it can lead only to cold-war controversy otherwise." See United Nations, General Assembly, Fifteenth Session, Part I, *Official Records,* Vol. 1, 906th plenary meeting, agenda item 9 (17 October 1960) (New York, 1961), p. 751.

[30] *Lok Sabha Debates,* Third Series, Vol. XXI, No. 26 Fifth Session (September 17, 1963) (New Delhi: Lok Sabha Secretariat, 1963), column 6636.

[31] I.C.W.A. Study, *op. cit.,* p. 41.

cized such a procedure because the Assembly would be challenging the very basis of the Security Council. He pointed out that "if amendments were necessary, they would have to obtain the requisite majority in the General Assembly and then be submitted to the members of the Security Council."[32] He offered a different formula, more in line with India's view, to consider Charter amendment on the basis of great power cooperation. He suggested that the United States, the Soviet Union, the United Kingdom and France, with or without the addition of some other states chosen unanimously by the four great powers, propose a solution to expand the councils of the United Nations at the Sixteenth Session of the General Assembly.[33]

INDIA'S ATTEMPTS TO AMEND THE CHARTER:
A POSITIVE POLICY

India's policy towards amending the United Nations Charter was not entirely a negative one. While consistently opposing Western efforts to amend the Charter India persistently attempted to bring changes in the Charter. India's desire to reduce Western domination over the United Nations led her to advocate changes in the structure of the United Nations in a way that would give greater representation to India and other Afro-Asian states.

Referring to an Argentine proposal to expand the membership of the Economic and Social Council, Mr. Kaul maintained that an increase in the membership of the Council would not provide an answer to the lack of balanced geographical distribution within the Council. He thought that Europe and Australia were over-represented, while Asia and the Middle East were under-represented. He felt

[32] United Nations, General Assembly, Fifteenth Session, *Official Records,* Special Political Committee, agenda item 23 (4 November 1963), (New York, 1964), p. 78.
[33] *Ibid.*

that a fairer geographical distribution appeared extremely necessary.[34] When a proposal was made in 1956 to expand the membership of the Security Council, Mr. Menon agreed that there was a case for the enlargement of the Council. He argued that the Security Council as it was then constituted was very ill-balanced and the mere addition of two more members, instead of correcting that imbalance, would accentuate it.[35] He contended that the whole of the enlargement should go to Asia to offset the existing imbalance and to make the Security Council more representative.[36] He explained that "these proposals do not achieve the purpose for which they have been put forward, namely, to provide more balanced representation. They increase the imbalance, they do not provide for the representation of a large number of small countries; they would in effect neglect the claims of Africa."[37] Opposing the proposals, Mr. Menon remarked

[34] United Nations, General Assembly, Second Session, *Official Records*, Joint Committee of the Second and Third Committees, 19th Meeting (October 23, 1947), p. 39. Mr. Shiva Rao thought in 1948 that the region to which Ceylon belonged was "as yet inadequately represented in the United Nations." See United Nations, General Assembly, Third Session, Part I, *Official Records*, 176th plenary meeting (8 December 1948) (Paris, 1949), pp. 784-5. Mr. Kondapi felt that Asia did not have effective representation in the United Nations. See Kondapi, *op. cit.*, p. 713. Mr. Krishna Menon held that there was inadequate representation of Asia in committees and councils of the United Nations and he desired broader representation to Asia in United Nations bodies. See United Nations, General Assembly, Ninth Session, *Official Records*, 492nd plenary meeting, agenda item 9 (6 October 1954) (New York, 1955), p. 232. See *The New York Times*, September 29, 1953, p. 3. See also "Membership of Economic and Social Council," *United Nations Weekly Bulletin*, Vol. III, No. 19 (November 4, 1947), p. 605.

[35] United Nations, General Assembly, Eleventh Session, *Official Records*, 622nd plenary meeting, agenda item 56 (17 December 1956) (New York, 1957), pp. 717-718.

[36] *Ibid.*, p. 718. He desired the enlargement and the allocation of seats of the Security Council on the basis of population, geography and group factors. *Ibid.*, pp. 718-719.

[37] United Nations, General Assembly, Eleventh Session, *Official Records*, 629th plenary meeting, agenda item 56 (20 December 1956) (New York, 1957), p. 772.

that "it creates, not only in the delegations here, but in our countries, the feeling that the United Nations is still a Western alliance."[38]

In 1959, Indian spokesmen favored an expansion in the membership of the Security Council and the Economic and Social Council but desired to achieve the objective with caution. Mr. Jha observed that "it was only right that both the composition of those organs and the expression of views therein should reflect the existing composition of the organization. He felt, however, that any increase should be qualitative and quantitative, and should lead to an equitable geographical distribution."[39] He explained that "there was a need not merely for an increase in membership of the principal organs proportionate to the increase in membership of the organization, but also for a rectification in the broadest sense of the maldistribution of membership."[40] Mr. Menon again expressed a desire to see the structure of the two councils correspond better to geographical and political realities in the world.[41]

Favoring changes in the structure of the United Nations, Mr. Nehru said in 1960 that "the Security Council did not now fairly represent the UN or the world as there should be a larger measure of consultation between different viewpoints at the top where the relatively 'simple organization'

[38] *Ibid.*, p. 771. Mr. Menon thought that the acceptance of such a proposition would introduce into the United Nations the idea that "we have a position of inferiority, a position of less potency, less requirement and less capacity to contribute to international well-being." *Ibid.*, p. 772.

[39] United Nations, General Assembly, Fourteenth Session, *Official Records,* Special Political Committee, 130th meeting, agenda item 19, 20 and 21 (15 October 1959) (New York, 1960), p. 13.

[40] *Ibid.* Mr. Jha complained that there was "gross under-representation of the Asian and African states in the Security Council and the Economic and Social Council." *Ibid.*

[41] United Nations, General Assembly, Fifteenth Session, *Official Records,* Special Political Committee, 191st meeting agenda item 23 (4 November 1960) (New York, 1961), p. 78.

was not suitable for handling the bigger and bigger jobs that the United Nations was given to do."[42] In 1960 India and other non-aligned states proposed that the United Nations revise its Charter "to expand the membership of the Security Council and the Economic and Social Council . . . bearing in mind equitable regional distribution."[43]

At the Eighteenth Session of the General Assembly India enthusiastically took an active part in the deliberations and negotiations dealing with Charter amendment. India supported proposals in the structure of the United Nations and introduced draft resolutions on behalf of fifty-four other sponsors. India and the other sponsors believed that "their cause was just and that the time was ripe to remedy the situation arising out of inequitable and unbalanced representation in the principal Councils of the United Nations, and the proposals were fair and equitable to all groups."[44] Expressing gratification at the adoption of the proposals by the General Assembly, Mr. Mishra of the Indian delegation stated that the proposals were "motivated by the desire to

[42] *The Times,* (London, October 22, 1960), p. 4. Mr. Nehru called for changes in the constitution of the Security Council "to make it more in tune with world realities, particularly in Asia and Africa." *Ibid.,* November 29, 1960, p. 10. See also Nehru, *India's Foreign Policy, op. cit.,* pp. 179, 180, 217-218. He reiterated in 1963 that the United Nations and the Security Council were "out of date" with the realities of the world and felt that changes were necessary. See *Lok Sabha Debates,* Third Series, Vol. XXI, No. 26 Fifth Session, (September 17, 1963) (New Delhi: Lok Sabha Secretariat, 1963), Column 6636. Mr. Menon thought that the lack of reorganization of the Security Council landed the United Nations in "plenty of difficulties." See United Nations, General Assembly Eleventh Session, *Official Record,* 622nd plenary meeting, agenda item 56 (17 December 1956) (New York, 1957), p. 719.

[43] *Facts on File Year Book 1961,* Vol. 21, No. 1090 (September 14-20, 1961), p. 344 A.

[44] United Nations, General Assembly, Eighteenth Session, *Official Records,* Vol. III, 1285th plenary meeting, agenda items 81, 82 and 12 (17 December 1963) (New York, 1964), p. 16. See also "India and Twenty Years of UN," *India News,* July 25, 1965, p. 5.

correct the imbalance by justice and fair play."[45] The sponsors explained that "the various organs of the United Nations should reflect more closely the increased membership of the Asian and African states in the organization."[46] Mr. Mishra said that "his delegation had been trying for years to get the Assembly to approve amendments to the Charter in order to give equitable representation to the African and Asian countries."[47] He hoped that members of the United Nations "would respect the wishes of the General Assembly expressed by such an overwhelming majority."[48] Mr. Swaran Singh thought that an expanded Security Council and an expanded Economic and Social Council would be much more representative and such an expansion would "serve to give them a broader base by including a larger number of African and Asian and other developing countries."[49] Mr. Ashok B. Bhadkamkar maintained that India's objective of securing equitable representation was to "achieve the best possible application in practice of the ideas of Charter."[50]

An observer on India's policy towards Charter revision concluded that during the first ten years whenever the question of charter revision was taken up "India was indifferent, and sometimes even indignant."[51] An examination of India's

[45] *Ibid.*

[46] United Nations, General Assembly, Eighteenth Session, *Official Records,* Annexes, Vol. III, agenda items 81, 82 and 12 (Documents A/5519 and A/5520) (New York, 1964), p. 2.

[47] "General Assembly Resolutions on Organizational Changes," *United Nations Review,* Vol. II, No. 3 (March 1964), p. 42.

[48] *Ibid.* Mr. Swaran Singh also expressed the same hope in 1964.

[49] United Nations, General Assembly, Nineteenth Session, *Official Records,* Vol. II, 1301st plenary meeting, item 9 of the provisional agenda (14 December 1964) (New York, 1965), p. 12.

[50] Rai, "Indian Attitude Towards Revision of the United Nations Charter-11," *op. cit.,* p. 109, citing United Nations (Document A/AC 81/SR 8), p. 11.

[51] Rai, "India's Attitude Towards the Revision of the United Nations Charter-1," *Foreign Affairs Reports* (India), XIV (June, 1965), p. 84.

policy, toward amending the United Nations Charter, revealed the invalidity of Rai's conclusion. While India was indifferent and indignant towards Western proposals, she steadfastly, although cautiously, attempted to bring changes in the Charter. India's coolness towards Western proposals stemmed from her desire to prevent the enhancement of Western domination over the United Nations. To some extent India's policy towards amending the Charter depended on the attitude of the great powers. Whenever the great-power confrontation on the issue of Charter amendment was serious India slackened her efforts at amending the Charter, and whenever the great-power confrontation on the issue receded India strove vigorously to revise the Charter and to make the United Nations an institution reflecting the geographical distribution of its membership. Besides India's stress on the "toning down" of the cold war, a vital factor that determined her policy on Charter revision was her conception of the United Nations and her desire to secure a better position for India in the Councils of the United Nations. India's persistence in 1963 to bring changes in the Charter, in the presence of American abstention, British coolness, French disapproval and Soviet objections, would seem to suggest that she determined to realize her conception of the United Nations as a broad based international organization reflecting the world as it was. The desire of Indian leaders to reduce the imbalance in the United Nations led them to make persistent efforts to amend the Charter in a way which would make its structure more balanced and its councils more representative in composition. Indians felt that an equitable distribution of representation, on geographical basis, in the councils of the United Nations would provide them greater opportunities for participation in those bodies.

3

India's Anti-Colonial Policy
at the United Nations

As has been noted, the freedom of dependent peoples has
been one of the objectives of Indian foreign policy. India's
policy makers felt that, having themselves won freedom from
colonial rule, they should naturally support the aspirations
of colonial people for self-determination. Prime Minister
Indira Gandhi said that "we, who have recently gained
independence from colonial rule, cannot for a moment forget
the sad plight and anguish under which our brothers and
sisters exist" in Asia, Africa and Latin America.[1] In the

[1] *India News,* April 29, 1966, p. 6, Mr. Lal Bahadur Shastri, Mrs.
Gandhi's predeccessor, expressed the same view and pledged that India
would consider it her moral duty to lend every support to the ending of
colonialism and imperialism so that all peoples everywhere would be free
to mold their own destiny. See *India News,* January 21, 1965, p. 5. This

same vein Foreign Minister Swaran Singh stated that "having ourselves waged a struggle against colonialism, we are passionately devoted to the elimination of colonial rule everywhere at the earliest possible date."[2] Indian delegates at the United Nations vigorously championed the cause of dependent people and invoked the organization to secure independence for those who were not yet free.

India's objective of liquidating colonialism was beyond doubt. Mr. Swaran Singh pledged that India would continue to support the colonial peoples to equality and independence until the last vestige of colonialism was removed.[3] India's uncompromising position on colonialism was firmly expressed by Mr. Menon in 1959. He insisted that "colonialism must end even if the colonialism is a benevolent one."[4] In 1965 Mr. G. Parthasarathi, India's Permanent Representative at the UN, declared that "India was passionately dedicated to the task of rapid and total eradication of

self-imposed obligation was enunciated by Mr. Nehru in 1948 when he stated that "we in Asia, who have ourselves suffered all these evils of colonialism and of imperial domination, have committed ourselves inevitably to the freedom of every other colonial country" quoted in United Nations, General Assembly, Eighteenth Session, *Official Records*, Vol. III, 1272nd plenary meeting, agenda item 23 (4 December 1963), p. 7. For similar expressions on India's self-imposed obligation see I.C.W.A. Study, *op. cit.*, p. 76; Ramu, *op. cit.*, p. 14.

[2] United Nations, General Assembly, Nineteenth Session, *Official Records*, Vol. 11, 1301st plenary meeting, agenda item 9 (14 December 1964) (New York, 1965), p. 12.

[3] *Lok Sabha Debates,* Third Series, Vol. XXXIV, No. 15, Ninth Session, (September 24, 1964) (New Delhi: Lok Sabha Secretariat, 1964), column 3795.

[4] United Nations, General Assembly, Fourteenth Session, *Official Records*, 823rd plenary meeting, agenda item 9 (October 6, 1959) (New York, 1960), p. 422. Mr. C. S. Jha declared that India was uncompromisingly anti-colonialist. See United Nations, General Assembly, Sixteenth Session, *Official Records*, Vol. 111, 1096th plenary meeting, agenda item 27 (25 January, 1962) (New York, 1963), p. 1271. Reverend J. d'Souza regarded self-determination as a pre-requisite of all other fundamental rights and that good government was no substitute for self-government. See United Nations, General Assembly, Tenth Session, *Official Records,* Third Committee, 651st meeting, agenda item 28 (3 November 1955) (New York, 1956), p. 135.

colonialism."[5] India considered colonialism an "evil" and threw her support and sympathies on the side of subject peoples.

NATURE OF INDIA'S ANTI-COLONIAL POLICY

Indians appreciated and admonished the policies of colonial powers. India's anti-colonial policy was reciprocative in the sense that it was a reaction to the policies adopted by the colonial governments. The extent of moderation or extremism in India's anti-colonialism depended on, what Indians viewed to be, the degree of liberalism or repression practiced by the colonial powers. A colonial country's determination to hold on to its colonial possessions met India's hostility, and an enlightened colonial policy with the ultimate objective of granting independence won India's praise. Whenever a colonial power showed accommodation Indians reciprocated with sympathy. As early as 1948 Mr. C. S. Jha expounded this reciprocal approach when he stated that India was prepared to show the utmost consideration for views held by the administering powers and she expected response from them commensurate with her reasonableness.[6]

MODERATION AND EXTREMISM IN INDIA'S ANTI-COLONIALISM

During the First Session of the General Assembly Mrs. Vijaya Lakshmi Pandit observed that problems which were the outgrowth of empire were the concern of the United Nations. She said that India looked to the United Nations to give the dependent peoples faith and hope and a promise

[5] "General Debate-Twentieth Session," *United Nations Monthly Chronicle*, Vol. 11, No. 10 (November 1965), p. 5.

[6] United Nations, General Assembly, Third Session, Part I, Fourth Committee, 72nd meeting (5 November 1948) (Paris, 1949), p. 251.

that their liberation was at hand.[7] There was an inkling of idealism in India's policy towards colonialism. In 1946, the Indian delegation desired trusteeship for all dependent areas and favored the setting up of appropriate time limits for independence in each of the trusteeship agreements.[8] Although India preferred direct United Nations trusteeship,[9] she agreed, in principle, to the administration of trust territories by individual states, the Indian delegation insisted on close supervision by the United Nations of the administration of Trust Territories, the attainment of independence by the Territories at the earliest possible time, the prevention of racial discrimination and the observance of the Trusteeship Agreements by the Administering Authorities in a broad and liberal spirit.[10] In accordance with this position Mr. V. K. Krishna Menon moved amendments to the proposed Trusteeship Agreement for Western Samoa to specify that in

[7] United Nations, General Assembly, First Session, Second Part, *Official Records,* 57th plenary meeting (25 October 1946) (New York, 1946), pp. 732-733.

[8] United Nations, General Assembly, First Session, Second Part, *Official Records,* Annex IV (New York, 1946), p. 1552. Mr. A. D. Mani thought that fixing a time limit over trusteeship would lead to the attainment of "right psychological frame of mind" for a transfer of power. See United Nations, General Assembly, Sixth Session, *Official Records,* Fourth Committee, 240th meeting, item 12 (9 January 1952) (Paris, 1952), p. 261.

[9] United Nations, General Assembly, First Session, Second Part, *Official Records,* Fourth Committee, Annex 12 b (Document A/C 4/33) (New York, 1946), p. 199. However, India realized, in later years, the impracticability of having the United Nations as Administering Authority. See United Nations, General Assembly, Eighth Session, *Official Records,* Fourth Committee, 390th meeting, item 13 (3 December 1953) (New York, 1953), p. 506.

[10] United Nations, General Assembly, Third Session, First Part, *Official Records,* Fourth Committee, 61st meeting (19 October 1948) (Paris, 1948), p. 100. India considered the advancement of the welfare of the inhabitants was another major objective of trusteeship. See United Nations, General Assembly, Fourth Session, *Official Records,* 222nd plenary meeting (21 September 1949) (Lake Success, 1949), p. 10. See also United Nations, General Assembly, Thirteenth Session, *Official Records,* Fourth Committee, 834th meeting, agenda item 36 (8 December 1958) (New York, 1958), p. 498.

Samoa decisions would be taken by local popular government and that there would not be any racial discrimination
in the Trust Territory. However, on hearing the assurances
given by the representative of New Zealand, Mr. Menon
expressed his satisfaction and withdrew his amendments.[11]

During the First Session India displayed moderation on
colonial issues at the United Nations. In 1946, Mr. Maharaj
Singh paid tribute to the British administration of Tanganyika and Mr. Menon was glad to hear that Britain did not
claim sovereignty over that territory.[12] In 1949, India
adopted a conciliatory approach with regard to a series of
proposals on political advancement in Trust Territories because she was "animated by a profound desire for the peaceful settlement of all international problems and firmly
believed in the value of patient and persistent negotiation."[13]
While demanding self-government to subject peoples, India's
Reverend Jerome d'Souza displayed a responsible position.
Reverend Jerome d'Souza recognized that there must be
some degree of educational progress before self-government
became feasible.[14]

[11] United Nations, General Assembly, First Session, Second Part, *Official Records,* Fourth Committee, Part 11, 8th meeting (25 November 1946)
(New York, 1946), p. 58.

[12] *Ibid.,* pp. 141, 211. In 1954 Mr. Menon hailed the United Kingdom's
decision to provide equality of representation in the new Tanganyika legislature as in the background of colonial practice, a "great advance." See
United Nations, General Assembly, Ninth Session, *Official Records,* 492nd
plenary meeting, agenda item 9 (6 October 1954) (New York, 1954), p.
227.

[13] United Nations, General Assembly, Fourth Session, *Official Records,*
239th plenary meeting (15 November 1949) (Lake Success, 1949), p.
176.

[14] United Nations, General Assembly, Fourth Session, *Official Records,*
Fourth Committee, 101st meeting (17 October 1949) (Lake Success,
1949), p. 60. In 1952 Mr. A. B. Pant also thought that "not all dependent
peoples were sufficiently mature for immediate freedom." See United
Nations, General Assembly, Sixth Session, *Official Records,* Fourth Committee, 242nd meeting, item 36 (10 January 1952) (Paris, 1952), p. 279.
India's demand for the transmission of political information to enable a

India's demand for information on Non-Self-Governing Territories was couched in cordial language whenever an Administering Power showed signs of submitting such information. In 1949, B. Shiva Rao stated that the Administering Powers should be encouraged to transmit information on Non-Self-Governing Territories on their progress and development and noted with satisfaction the liberal attitude of the United States and Denmark for not withholding any information on the Territories administered by them.[15] He reiterated several times India's desire to establish a committee to consider the information transmitted by the Administering Powers to defend the interests of the inhabitants and to make recommendations in the functional fields.[16]

While exhibiting temperance over several colonial issues, Indian delegates adopted a hostile posture towards the Netherlands. Dr. P. P. Pillai bitterly attacked the colonial power and said that "the very fact that foreign armies were functioning on Asian soil was itself an outrage against sentiment prevailing not only in India but throughout the whole

---

proper discussion of political advancement by the Fourth Committee came in 1954. See United Nations, General Assembly, Ninth Session, *Official Records*, Fourth Committee, 412th meeting, agenda item 31 (25 October 1954) (New York, 1954), p. 106.

[15] United Nations, General Assembly, Fourth Session, *Official Records*, Fourth Committee, 109th meeting (27 October 1949) (Lake Success, 1949), p. 139. In 1951 Mr. A. B. Pant congratulated the Administering Powers for having transmitted the information and for having participated in the discussions of the Special Committee in the most "laudable spirit of cooperation." See United Nations, General Assembly, Sixth Session. *Official Records*, Fourth Committee, 205th meeting (19 November 1951) (Paris, 1951), p. 24.

[16] *Ibid.*, 121st meeting (10 November 1949), p. 166. See also United Nations, General Assembly, Fifth Session, *Official Records*, Fourth Committee, 179th meeting (16 November 1950) (Lake Success, 1950), p. 231. For India's role in setting up the Committee on Information and in utilizing that committee to promote the interests of dependent peoples see, Usha Sud, "Committee on Information from Non-Self-Governing Territories: Its role in the promotion of self-determination of Colonial Peoples," *International Studies* (New Delhi), Vol. VII, No. 2 (October 1965), pp. 311-336.

of Asia."[17] Although the Indonesian question was on the agenda of the Security Council, in 1949 India insisted, contrary to its general practice, that the General Assembly consider the issue to help find a peaceful solution.[18]

France's suppression of the nationalist movement in Tunisia in 1952 brought India's condemnation of the French government. Madame Pandit demanded the United Nations take steps "to ensure respect for the principle of the right of peoples to self-determination, in accordance with both the Charter and present day realities."[19] When the Security Council decided not to hear the French-Tunisian dispute, Mr. Nehru expressed his disappointment and remarked that "the United Nations has swerved from its original moorings and gradually become a protector of colonialism."[20] France's objection to the General Assembly's consideration of Tunisian question on the ground that it was a domestic matter led Mr. Menon to argue that Tunisia was a "formerly independent nation which the French authorities, by abusing Tunisia's hospitality, had subjected to a tutelage from which today it must be set free."[21] India held France responsible for the troubles in Tunisia and wanted the French government to follow a conciliatory policy. Madame Pandit appealed to France to desist from measures of repression and violence against the Tunisian people and to enter into nego-

[17] "Council Takes Further Action on Indonesia," *United Nations Weekly Bulletin,* Vol. 3, No. 10 (September 2, 1947), p. 298. Berkes and Bedi considered India's role on the Indonesian question as an "aggressive" and a "radical" one. See Berkes and Bedi, *op. cit.,* p. 203.

[18] "Indonesia Before the Assembly," *United Nations Weekly Bulletin,* Vol. 6, No. 9 (May 1, 1949), p. 452.

[19] United Nations, General Assembly, Seventh Session, *Official Records,* First Committee, 540th meeting, item 60 (9 December 1952) (New York, 1952), p. 213.

[20] Nehru, *Jawaharla Nehru's Speeches 1949-1953, op. cit.,* p. 224.

[21] United Nations, General Assembly, Seventh Session, *Official Records,* First Committee, 546th meeting (12 December 1952) (New York, 1952), p. 268.

tiations with the representatives of the people.[22] India's condemnation of French colonial policy did not inhibit her from commending the enlightened colonial policy of the United Kingdom. Mr. A. B. Pant recognized that much serious effort had been made in the direction of self-rule in the Trust Territories under the United Kingdom and he welcomed the British Governments' intention "to lead those Territories to full self-government."[23] There was both sympathy and antipathy in India's anti-colonial policy simultaneously operating in two directions. Madame Pandit expressed this varied Indian reaction to different colonial policies when she stated that it could be said "to the credit of some of the imperial powers that the process of independence was happily consummated in some countries in an atmosphere free from bitterness and violence; but in Africa we see a spectacle of an entrenched colonialism turning its back upon the swelling tide of nationalism. This refusal to recognize the lessons of history and the laws of human evolution is producing a situation of acute tension and instability."[24]

[22] United Nations, General Assembly, Seventh Session, *Official Records,* 404th plenary meeting, agenda item 60 (17 December 1952) (New York, 1953), p. 378. Mr. Menon held the same view on the question of Morocco and wanted the General Assembly to ask the parties concerned to enter into negotiations to reach a peaceful settlement. He contended that the United Nations was competent to invite the parties to undertake negotiations. See United Nations, General Assembly, Seventh Session, *Official Records,* First Committee, 550th meeting (16 December 1952) (New York, 1953), p. 299.

[23] United Nations, General Assembly, Seventh Session, *Official Records,* Fourth Committee, 280th meeting, item 12 (21 November 1952) (New York, 1953), p. 213. Mr. Pant expressed in 1951 a similar appreciation of British policy towards non-self-govening Territories and complimented the United Kingdom for encouraging the indigenous Ugandans to participate actively in the economic activities of their country. See United Nations, General Assembly, Sixth Session, *Official Records,* Fourth Committee, 211th meeting (26 November 1951) (New York, 1952), p. 59.

[24] United Nations, General Assembly, Seventh Session, *Official Records,* 404th plenary meeting, agenda item 60 (17 December 1952) (New York, 1954), p. 378.

In 1953, Mr. Rajeswar Dayal of the Indian delegation regretted the French decision not to take part in the debate on Morocco and charged that France, in place of negotiation, had used the language of force. He argued that "France could not create an atmosphere of respect and mutual confidence by demonstrations of military power and repressive measures against the Istiqlal party."[25] While questioning the French contention that her North African Territories were a part of France, India expressed gratification at Denmark's announcement that "Greenland had reached a stage of self-government and had become an integral part of Denmark."[26]

A change in French policy towards Tunisia in 1954 brought a corresponding change in India's anti-colonial policy. When France adopted a liberal policy in Tunisia, India responded with understanding and requested the General Assembly to postpone consideration of the Tunisian question. Mr. Menon thought that the new French approach would lead to a satisfactory settlement.[27] Lauding New

[25] United Nations, General Assembly, Eighth Session, *Official Records,* First Committee, 633rd meeting, item 57 (13 October 1953) (New York, 1954), p. 40.

[26] United Nations, General Assembly, Ninth Session, *Official Records,* Fourth Committee, 412th meeting, agenda item 31 (25 October 1954) (New York, 1955), p. 106. Although India contended that the General Assembly should be satisfied about the termination of trusteeship and indicated that it might be valuable for the United Nations to visit territories which were about to attain independence, she felt that it was hardly appropriate in the case of Greenland because Denmark supplied all the information in detail. See United Nations, General Assembly, Ninth Session, *Official Records,* Fourth Committee, 427th meeting, item 32 (10 November 1954) (New York, 1955), p. 206. India maintained that an Administering Power could not unilaterally terminate or change the status of trusteeship and for any such action the approval of the United Nations was required. See United Nations, General Assembly, Eleventh Session, *Official Records,* Fourth Committee, 597th meeting, agenda item 39 (11 January 1957) (New York, 1958), p. 241. See also United Nations, General Assembly, Fifteenth Session, Part 1. *Official Records,* Vol. 2, 944th plenary meeting, agenda item 87 (13 December 1960), (New York, 1961), p. 1243.

[27] United Nations, General Assembly, Ninth Session, *Official Records,* 492nd plenary meeting, agenda item 9 (6 October 1954) (New York,

Zealand's administration of Western Samoa, he stated: "As regards the Trust Territories, I think this Assembly would want to—and I feel we ought to—pay high tribute to that great little country of New Zealand for the very bold and very imaginative task . . . it has undertaken in Western Samoa. This is one region of the world in which, although one nation rules another, yet there is a greater sense of equality than anywhere else. The Administering Authority has never in word, in deed, or in sentiment, expressed the idea that this territory is New Zealand Samoa, they speak about Western Samoa."[28]

During the Tenth Session, Mr. Krishna Menon, insisting that the General Assembly should consider the Algerian question, argued that the consideration of the issue would not result in the violation of Article 2, paragraph 7, of the Charter.[29] He believed that public discussion of complex problems was likely to assist in finding solutions. He emphasized the fact that on colonial issues India's relations with France were concerned with "finding ways and means of settling difficulties rather than of creating them."[30] Mr.

1955), p. 226. Mr. Nehru said that India accorded full recognition to the wisdom and statesmanship of the French government. See Nehru, *India's Foreign Policy, op. cit.,* p. 505.

[28] *Ibid.,* p. 277. Indian spokesmen repeatedly praised the enlightened colonial rule of New Zealand over Western Samoa. See United Nations, General Assembly, Sixteenth Session, *Official Records,* Vol. 1, Fourth Committee, 1170th meeting, agenda item 48 (13 October 1961) (New York, 1962), p. 87.

[29] United Nations, General Assembly, Tenth Session, *Official Records,* 530th plenary meeting, agenda item 8 (30 September 1955) (New York, 1956), p. 190. He reiterated this position in 1960. See United Nations, General Assembly, Fifteenth Session, Part 1, *Official Records,* First Committee, 1132nd meeting, agenda item 71 (15 December 1960) (New York, 1962), p. 262. Mr. Menon maintained the same position on the Cyprus question and contended that the Assembly had total competence to call upon the parties to "enter into negotiations and unremittingly strive to bring about a settlement." See United Nations, General Assembly, Tenth Session, *Official Records,* 521st plenary meeting, agenda item 8 (23 September 1955) (New York, 1956), p. 62.

[30] *Ibid.,* 533rd plenary meeting, agenda item 9 (4 October 1955), p. 240.

Menon kept his promise by adopting moderation on French colonial policy in North Africa and by requesting the General Assembly not to consider the Algerian question at the Tenth Session.[31] India displayed both firmness and moderation in her stand over the Cyprus question in 1955.

A POLICY OF MODERATION

In 1956, Prime Minister Nehru recognized French difficulties over Algeria and sympathized with France. Nehru's belief that there was a recognition on the part of France that the Algerian claims have to be met led him to adopt moderation on the question. He stated that "it should be our endeavor to assist the forces which stand for a constructive settlement by urging the fuller recognition of national aspirations and at the same time by not encouraging hatred and violence on either side."[32] While maintaining a policy of moderation over French colonial policy, India adopted a policy of appreciation towards British colonial policy. When Britain conveyed her intention to grant independence to the

[31] United Nations, General Assembly, Tenth Session, *Official Records, First Committee,* 795th meeting (25 November 1955) (New York, 1955), p. 203. According to Kamath, India helped France by prevailing upon the Afro-Asians to approach the Algerian question with moderation. See M. Y. Kamath, "India at the United Nations," *United Asia,* Vol. 9 (September 1957) p. 225. Mr. Menon noted that the United Nations endeavored to serve as a center for harmonizing conflicting interests on the Moroccan question and thought that the United Nations was entitled to commendation for having displayed a moderation in the consideration of the problem. See United Nations, General Assembly, Tenth Session, *Official Records,* First Committee, 797th meeting, agenda item 58 (28 November 1955) (New York, 1955), p. 210.

[32] Nehru, *India's Foreign Policy, op. cit.,* p. 506. It was significant that India did not even join the Afro-Asians in requesting the inclusion of Algerian question on the agenda of the Eleventh Session. When France participated in the discussion on Algeria, Mr. Menon expressed his satisfaction and thought that such attitude augured well for the future. See United Nations, General Assembly, Eleventh Session, *Official Records,* First Committee, 844th meeting, agenda item 62 (12 February 1957) (New York, 1957), p. 199.

Gold Coast, Mr. Krishna Menon expressed his admiration of the United Kingdom. He said that "here is an imperial country, to a very large extent steeped in the attributes of empire, but also imbued with the traditions of liberal administration, coming forward for the first time and saying: 'We want to release these people from tutelage whom we governed as a colonial power and afterwards as custodians.' "[33] He observed that an imperial country had shown "the height of its greatness by the magnanimity of the abandonment of empire."[34]

The Franco-Indian harmony over French colonial policy showed signs of strain when France attempted to suppress the nationalist movement in Algeria. In July 1958 India and twenty-three Afro-Asian countries, requesting the General Assembly to consider the Algerian issue, stated that "the hostilities in Algeria continue unabated causing increasing suffering and loss of human life."[35] Nehru remarked that "we have been greatly distressed by the very cruel repression of that (nationalist) movement in Algeria by the French authorities and armies. Our sympathies are with the people of Algeria."[36] However, with signs of a liberal colonial

[33] United Nations, General Assembly, Eleventh Session, *Official Records,* Vol. 11, 619th plenary meeting, agenda item 39 (13 December 1956) (New York, 1956), p. 682. Mr. Menon expressed similar sentiments in 1955. See United Nations, General Assembly, Tenth Session, *Official Records,* 533rd plenary meeting, agenda item 9 (4 October 1955) (New York 1955), p. 241. He mentioned the names of several British administrators and praised them. *Ibid.* He acknowledged that liberal administrations in dependent territories yielded "rich harvests and good results." Referring to the British administration over Togoland he said that the United Nations owed "a debt of gratitude to the Administering Authority." See United Nations, General Assembly, Tenth Session, *Official Records,* 556th plenary meeting, agenda item 35 (15 December 1955) (New York, 1955), p. 456.

[34] *Ibid.*

[35] United Nations, General Assembly, Thirteenth Session, *Official Records,* Annexes, agenda item 63 (Doc. A/3853, 16 July 1958), p. 2.

[36] Nehru, *India's Foreign Policy, op. cit.,* p. 509.

policy on the part of General de Gaulle's government, India exhibited forbearance in her attitude towards France. Mr. Krishna Menon believed that General de Gaulle's speeches implied France's desire to grant freedom to Algeria and said that such implications augured well for the future.[37] Mr. J. Rameswar Rao, commending the French administration over Togoland, said that "India appreciated the vision and wisdom of France, which in the traditions of its great liberal ideas was leading the people of Togoland to equality and freedom."[38] Expressing the reciprocative factor in India's anti-colonialism, Mr. Menon stated that "since we are critical of colonial rule, we are only happy to pay our tribute to the metropolitan countries, which, for one reason or another, and not the least for liberal and humanitarian reasons, have contributed towards the liberation" of the colonial territories.[39] Indian delegates were pleased by Belgium's announcement offering independence to the Congo and Britain's decision to grant freedom to Cyprus and Nigeria.[40]

[37] United Nations, General Assembly, Thirteenth Session, *Official Records,* First Committee, 1022nd meeting, agenda item 63 (13 December 1958) (New York, 1958), p. 374.

[38] United Nations, General Assembly, Thirteenth Session, *Official Records,* Fourth Committee 787th meeting, agenda item 40 (6 November 1958 (New York, 1958), p. 225. Mr. Menon thought that French policy over Guinea indicated "liberation" in the French Empire. See United Nations, General Assembly, Thirteenth Session, *Official Records,* 774th plenary meeting, agenda item 9 (7 October 1958) (New York, 1958), p. 368. When France adopted a liberal policy over the French Cameroons, India expressed her satisfaction of French policy and opposed the extreme demands of the Africans. India dissuaded the Africans and helped in putting across a resolution acceptable to France. See *The New York Times* March 4, 1959, p. 7. See also "Noble Motives," *The Reporter,* Vol. 21 (November 12, 1959), p. 6.

[39] United Nations, General Assembly, Thirteenth Session, *Official Records,* 774th plenary meeting, agenda item 9 (7 October 1958) (New York, 1958), p. 367.

[40] United Nations, General Assembly, Fourteenth Session, *Official Records,* 823rd plenary meeting, agenda item 9 (6 October 1959) (New York, 1959), p. 422.

In 1959, Mr. R. Venkatarman, expressing satisfaction with New Zealand's discharge of its responsibility, regretted Belgium's refusal to transmit political information.[41] He thought that it was one of the greatest tragedies of the time that Angola and Mozambique were not considered non-self-governing by the colonial power administering them and he wanted the United Nations to end that "manifestation of tyranny." He thanked the United States for transmitting information on political and constitutional developments in Hawaii and Alaska, and recognized that those two Territories had made great strides toward self-government. On behalf of his delegation he congratulated the United States "on its successful efforts in bringing those two Territories to a full measure of self-government."[42]

Generally India did not favor the setting up of target dates for terminating colonial rule. The sympathetic inclination towards their commonwealth colleagues led Indian spokesmen to discourage the fixing of a time limit for granting self-government to British administered Gold Coast[43] and

[41] United Nations, General Assembly, Fourteenth Session, *Official Records,* Fourth Committee, 970th meeting, agenda item 36 (25 November 1959) (New York, 1959), p. 516. He maintained that Spain and France should transmit information on their colonial possessions. See *Ibid.,* 981st meeting (2 December 1959), pp. 593-594.

[42] United Nations, General Assembly, Fourteenth Session, *Official Records,* Fourth Committee, 981st meeting, agenda item 36 (2 December 1959) (New York, 1959), p. 592.

[43] United Nations, General Assembly, Tenth Session, *Official Records,* Fourth Committee, 538th meeting, agenda item 35 (8 December 1955) (New York, 1956), p. 384. It should not be construed that India always praised British colonial policy and that India's commendation of British policy was taken for granted. Although India was more favorably inclined towards the colonial policy of Her Majesty's Government, India's response to British colonial policy, like its reaction to any other colonial policy, varied from case to case. In 1959, Mr. Venkataraman deplored the racial practices in the East African Territories administered by the United Kingdom. See United Nations, General Assembly, Fourteenth Session, *Official Records,* Fourth Committee, 970th meeting, agenda item 36 (25 November 1959) (New York, 1960), p. 516. In 1953, Mrs. Lakshmi Menon expressed apprehension at British policy in Central Africa and Kenya. See United Nations, General Assembly, Eighth Ses-

Australian administered New Guinea.[44] However, Indians did not have the same confidence in Belgian bona fides and their doubts led them to insist on the establishment of target dates for ending Belgian rule over Ruanda-Urundi.[45]

At the Fifteenth Session of the General Assembly, Mr. Krishna Menon stored in himself both brusqueness and friendliness for appropriate use as the occasion demanded. Promptly paying his tribute to the United Kingdom,[46] Mr. Menon bitterly attacked France and Portugal. He referred to reports about the existence of forced labor in the Portuguese territories bordering on slavery and said that France was attempting to subjugate the Algerians by force of arms.[47] However, when France exhibited signs of a liberalization in its policy India displayed understanding and friendliness.

---

sion, *Official Records,* Fourth Committee, 395th meeting, agenda item 32 (7 December 1953) (New York, 1954), p. 540. In 1965, Mr. Swaran Singh thought that British Guiana, Fizi and Mauritania were ripe for independence and charged that "the traditional divisive policies of the United Kingdom have resulted in creating tensions among the people thus retarding their emergence into freedom." See "General Debate— Twentieth Session," *United Nations Monthly Chronicle,* Vol. 11, No. 10 (November 1965), p. 120.

[44] United Nations, General Assembly, Eleventh Session, *Official Records,* Fourth Committee, 637th meeting, agenda item 13 (15 February 1957) (New York, 1958), p. 431.

[45] United Nations, General Assembly, Twelfth Session, *Official Records,* Fourth Committee, 722nd meeting, agenda item 13 (29 November 1957) (New York, 1958), p. 384. See also United Nations, General Assembly, Fourteenth Session, *Official Records,* Fourth Committee 945th meeting, agenda items 13 and 39 (10 November 1959) (New York, 1960), p. 338; and *Ibid.,* 954th meeting (16 November 1959), p. 412.

[46] United Nations, General Assembly, Fifteenth Session, Part 1, *Official Records,* Vol. 1, 906th plenary meeting, agenda item 9 (17 October 1960) (New York, 1961), p. 747.

[47] United Nations, General Assembly, Fifteenth Session, Part 1, *Official Records,* Vol. 2, 944th plenary meeting, agenda item 87 (13 December 1960) (New York, 1961), p. 1241. To Nehru the struggle in Algeria was a "Continuing tragedy of a brave people" fighting for independence. See *Ibid.,* Vol. 1, 882nd plenary meeting, agenda item 9 (3 October 1960), p. 328. In 1961, Mr. Menon supported the Algerian demand for full and complete independence. See United Nations, General Assembly, Sixteenth Session, *Official Records,* Vol. 1, 1025th plenary meeting, agenda item 9 (4 October 1961) (New York, 1962), p. 246.

Mr. C. S. Jha stated that India was well aware of the difficulties that France faced in Algeria. He paid tributes to General de Gaulle "for his steadfast adherence . . . to the principle of Algerian self-determination and independence."[48]

INDIA'S INTRANSIGENT ANTI-COLONIAL ROLE

While India was sympathetic toward French policy, her reaction to Portuguese colonial policy was one of hostility. Mr. Jha, deploring the Portuguese colonial system, said that it was characterized by much severity, depravity and degradation.[49] He called Portuguese colonialism the "most vicious and virulent" form of colonialism and insisted that it must go.[50] India and forty-one other countries charged that Portugal "continued its policy of merciless suppression, of mass killings and the blatant violation of the human rights and fundamental freedoms of the people of Angola."[51] Mr.

[48] United Nations, General Assembly, Sixteenth Session, *Official Records,* First Committee, 1223rd meeting, agenda item 80 (16 December 1961) (New York, 1962), p. 320.

[49] United Nations, General Assembly, Fifteenth Session, Part 11, *Official Records,* 992nd plenary meeting, agenda item 92 (20 April 1961), p. 425. He held that Portuguese rule over Goa was brutal and repressive. *Ibid.*

[50] United Nations, General Assembly, Sixteenth Session, *Official Records,* Vol. 111, 1096th plenary meeting, agenda item 27 (25 January 1962) (New York, 1962), p. 1269. Mr. Shastri expressed his firm opposition and his desire to end Portuguese colonialism. See Shastri, *op. cit.,* p. 102.

[51] United Nations, General Assembly, Sixteenth Session, *Official Records, Annexes,* Vol. 1, agenda item 27 (Document A/4816, 19 July 1961) (New York, 1962), p. 2. Alone of all the Afro-Asian countries, the Indian delegation requested in 1961 that the question of the non-compliance of Portugal with the Charter and with the resolutions of the General Assembly be placed on the agenda of the Sixteenth Session. In its request India charged that Portugal was carrying on atrocities and oppression with varying degrees of brutality. See *Ibid.,* Vol. 111, agenda item 79 (Document A/4841, 9 August 1961), p. 2. See also United Nations, Security Council, *Official Records,* 952nd meeting (7 June 1961) (New York, 1962), pp. 6-15. Machiavellian motives were attributed to

Menon condemned the Portuguese colonial system and stated that the Portuguese colonial rule was characterized by cruelty and repression, by police and army massacres, and by the use of napalm bombs on village people.[52] He referred to Portuguese contention that Goa was an integral part of Portugal and remarked that "Portugal was denying the homeland to the people to whom it really belonged."[53] Mr. Menon was critical of such a colonial policy and directed verbal diatribes at Portugal. Expressing India's attitude toward Portuguese position over Goa, he warned that "we as a state have not abjured the use of force. . . . And therefore if aggression continues forever, if our people are subjected to being shot in cold blood, if there is not civil liberty and if the peace and security of our land on the one hand and of the world as a whole is being endangered by the continuance of conflicts on our territory, no one has a right . . . to prevent a sovereign land like ours seeking to complete the liberation of our entire country."[54] Thus the ruthlessness of Portuguese rule incurred Mr. Menon's wrath and the degree of colonial repression determined the extent of India's aggressiveness in her anti-colonial outbursts. Mr. Jha maintained in 1962 that

India for such an intransigent position on Portuguese colonial policy in Africa. It was argued that by depicting the gloomy picture of Portuguese rule over Angola and by whipping public opinion against Portugal, India prepared an opportune ground to strike a blow against Portugal in Goa. See Royal Institute of International Affairs, *Survey of International Affairs 1961* (Oxford: Royal Institute of International Affairs, 1965), p. 448.

[52] United Nations, General Assembly, Sixteenth Session, *Official Records,* Vol. 1, 1025th plenary meeting, agenda item 9 (4 October 1961) (New York, 1962), p. 248.

[53] United Nations, General Assembly, Sixteenth Session, *Official Records,* Vol. 11, 1058th plenary meeting, agenda items 88 and 22 (20 November 1961) (New York, 1962), p. 714. Mr. Sahni held that the Portuguese contention that her colonies were an integral part of Portugal as a perverse political doctrine. See United Nations, General Assembly, Sixteenth Session, *Official Records,* Vol. 1, Fourth Committee, 1203rd meeting, agenda item 79 (9 November 1961) (New York, 1962), p. 293.

[54] *Ibid.* Within a month after this statement was made, India incorporated Goa in her territory.

the Afro-Asians were not making unreasonable charges against Portugal and pointed to the friendly relations that existed between Britain and France on the one hand and the states which were at one time under their rule. He observed: "Let it therefore not be said lightheartedly that the African and Asian countries in this (United Nations) Organization are carrying on some kind of crusade against the countries of the Western world or that it is a creed with them to oppose the West. . . . The truth is that those whose positions are more or less static and immovable regard and resent even moderate winds of change from Africa and Asia as a destructive hurricane. There is no doubt that, if Portugal were to act with the same wisdom which informed the actions of other colonial powers such as Britain and France, it would receive here the same understanding and sympathy as these other colonial powers, which have shown a capacity and readiness to adjust to changing times."[55]

At the Seventeenth Session India's attitude toward Portuguese policy went beyond condemnation. Indian delegates were extremely vituperative and carried on a vendetta against Portugal. Mr. Bhadkamkar referred to the Portuguese rule over Angola and said that "not only the conscience but the ire of mankind has been aroused by the continued perpetration of this foul tragedy in Angola."[56] He contended that the Portuguese claim over Angola was

[55] United Nations, General Assembly, Sixteenth Session, *Official Records,* Vol. 111, 1096th plenary meeting, agenda item 27 (25 January 1962) (New York, 1963), p. 1272.

[56] United Nations, General Assembly, Seventeenth Session, *Official Records,* Vol. 111, 1185th plenary meeting, agenda item 29 (6 December 1962) (New York, 1963), p. 1006. Mr. Bhadkamkar and other Afro-Asian delegates requested the General Assembly to consider the situation in Angola and to urge Portugal and the Angolan nationalists to undertake negotiations for reaching a settlement. See United Nations, General Assembly, Seventeenth Session, *Official Records, Annexes,* Vol. 111, agenda item 80 (Doc. A/4842, and Add. 1, 11 August 1961) (New York, 1963), p. 2.

"preposterous"[57] and such a claim deserved greater condemnation. He pungently pointed out that "Portugal has chosen to bury itself in its peculiarly medieval concept of the development of history and to embark on a path of violent and savage repression designed to achieve exactly the opposite of what otherwise could be a successful solution likely to have the most far-reaching consequences on future Portuguese history. . . . The colossal human misery involved in the butchery that has been the horrible affair has shaken mankind to its very core. . . . In the name of national prestige, Portugal is perpetrating the most barbarous and tyrannical policies on the people of its colony of Angola."[58] He favored the imposition of sanctions on Portugal to secure the compliance of the Portuguese government to the resolutions of the General Assembly.[59]

In 1963 while condemning Portugal, Mr. B. C. Chakravarty pointed to the commendable record of the United Kingdom in bringing its colonial territories to independence and expressed his "deep appreciation of the colonial policy of the United Kingdom."[60]

During the Nineteenth Session India's antagonism toward Portuguese colonialism persisted. India again denounced Portuguese refusal to cooperate with the Special Committee on colonialism and its continuous flouting of the United Nations resolutions. An Indian delegate bitterly remarked that "deplorable conditions continue to reign in the Portu-

[57] *Ibid.*

[58] *Ibid.*

[59] *Ibid.* Mr. Ashok Mehta thought that the Portuguese were "arrogant" and felt that the problem of Portuguese colonial rule could only be settled by decisive action, like the imposition of sanctions. See United Nations, General Assembly, Eighteenth Session, *Official Records,* Vol. 1, Fourth Committee, 1475th meeting, agenda item 23 (11 November 1963) (New York, 1964), p. 283.

[60] *Ibid.* United Nations, General Assembly, Eighteenth Session, *Official Records,* Vol. 111, 1272nd plenary meeting, agenda item 23 (4 December 1963) (New York, 1964), p. 7.

guese African colonies, where the struggle for freedom was being ruthlessly suppressed."[61] In 1964 Mr. Swaran Singh condemned the brutal repression of the people of Angola and Mozambique and considered it a challenge to the conscience and will of the United Nations.[62]

SOME MISLEADING OBSERVATIONS

Several misconceptions about India's anti-colonial policy seemed to exist in the writings of several scholars. After an examination of India's policy on colonial questions, Berkes and Bedi observed that "the uneven beginnings in the transformation of India's performance from that of a radical power to that of a conservative power"[63] was apparent. They explained: "By comparison, India's aggressive role regarding Indonesian independence nearly a decade before, and its vigilance regarding Tunisia and Morocco, were molding a tradition against which its behavior on the Algerian question might better be regarded as either an exception or a new departure. Taken in conjunction with a similar moderation on other colonial issues, the newer behavior seems to merit more than designation as a category of exceptions."[64]

[61] United Nations, General Assembly, Nineteenth Session, *Official Records*, Annexes, Vol. 1, Annex 8, Part 1 (Document A/5800/Rev. 1) (New York, 1966), p. 167.

[62] *Lok Sabha Debates,* Ninth Session, Third Series, Vol. XXXIV, No. 15 (September 25, 1964) (New Delhi: Lok Sabha Secretariat, 1964), column 3796.

[63] Berkes and Bedi, p. 203. Lord Birdwood seemed to hold a similar notion. However, he attributed India's extremism on colonialism to Soviet tactics. He thought that lately a change occurred in India's policy and said that India was a balancing influence on colonial questions at the United Nations, see Lord Birdwood, "The United Nations and Asia," *Royal Central Asian Society Journal,* Vol. XLVII (July-October, 1960), p. 188.

[64] *Ibid.,* p. 159. Palmer observed that India displayed moderation in her anti-colonial policy by supporting a policy of gradualism in granting independence to some dependent areas. See Norman D. Palmer, "Indian Attitude Toward Colonialism," *Orbis,* "A Quarterly Journal of World Affairs," published by The Foreign Research Institute of the University of Pennsylvania. Vol. 1, No. 2 (Summer 1957), p. 234.

India's anti-colonial policy had been basically consistent. It was erroneous to attribute that a transformation had occurred in India's anti-colonial policy. The argument that India's policy had moved from extremism to moderation through the years was not supported by facts. India was neither a radical power nor a conservative power but it was simply an Indian power, following an aggressive or a moderate policy in response to the policies pursued by the colonial powers. For instance India exhibited moderation on colonial issues in the early stages of the United Nations history and her anti-colonial policy reached its aggressive proportions when India took military action in Goa in 1961.

It was held that India resorted to extremism on colonial issues with a view to maintain the semblance of Asian unity. According to Werner Levi "the strength of Asian unity equals the strength of anti-Western feeling and is dependent on it. . . . India, eager to maintain the semblance of Asian unity in international councils, has to fall back therefore upon anti-Western feeling as a poor but still effective substitute."[65] India's policy on colonialism was not a negative one and she paid tributes whenever she was satisfied with the colonial policies of the Western powers. Levi had to explain why Mr. Nehru appreciated British and French policies on several occasions and Mr. Menon commended Denmark, New Zealand, France and the United Kingdom from time to time.

In the opinion of Gupta, India's anti-colonial policy was guided by a narrow concept of national interest. Gupta argued that Nehru's antipathy to French policy in Indo-

[65] Levi, "The Evolution of India's Foreign Policy," *op. cit.,* p. 132. It could be asked why some countries like Pakistan, Turkey and the Philippines that followed anti-colonialism did not engage in anti-Westernism. Perhaps a factor that influenced India's anti-colonial policy was her desire to maintain her influence in Afro-Asian countries. See *Royal Institute of International Affairs, op. cit.,* p. 448. See also *The New York Times,* December 24, 1961, Section VI, p. 4E.

China and North Africa might have been due to India's irritation at French refusal to withdraw from French "pockets in India."[66] He thought that India's anti-colonialism was tempered by the fact that India depended on the West for her economic development and military supplies.[67] It was true that India's policy toward colonialism was determined by her conception of her national interest. India's support to the demand for self-determination stemmed from her desire to promote her national interest.[68] But it must be emphasized that an element of condemnation, or lack of condemnation or commendation in India's anti-colonial policy developed as a response to the attitude adopted by the colonial powers.

India's anti-colonial policy varied from issue to issue in accordance with the varying policies and tactics of the colonial powers. Nehru's criticism of French colonial policy was a case in point. He bitterly attacked France in 1953, praised her in 1956 and 1957, condemned her in 1958 and appreciated her in later years. Whenever a colonial power pursued a liberal or repressive colonial policy India responded with a corresponding degree of commendation or condemnation. India's policy toward colonialism could very well have been termed as reciprocative anti-colonial policy.

[66] Gupta, *op. cit.*, p. 64. However, French withdrawal from the Indian sub-continent did not prevent India from condemning French policy in Algeria and India's criticism of France was as strong, if not stronger, in 1960 as it was in 1953.

[67] *Ibid.*, pp. 77, 78. This contention was refuted by Michael Brecher. See Brecher, *Nehru: A Political Biography, op. cit.*, p. 560.

[68] India championed the cause of dependent peoples with the objective of winning their good-will for she considered it to be too valuable an asset to have. See "Pandit Nehru's Foreign Policy," *The Economist*, Vol. 159 (July-December 1950), p. 273. In advocating the welfare of the non-self-governing people, Indian spokesmen had an eye on the educated minds in those territories and aimed to create a favorable opinion of India on them. See United Nations, General Assembly, Second Session, *Official Records*, Fourth Committee, 42nd meeting (11 October, 1947) (Lake Success, 1948), p. 47.

4

India and the United Nations
Peace-Keeping Forces

The United Nations peace-keeping operations enabled India to play an active role in the United Nations. India's desire to take part in the maintenance of peace and security led her to contribute men and material resources to various peace-keeping operations. India's desire to have a share in the maintenance of peace and security was expressed as early as 1946. The Indian delegation at the San Francisco Conference insisted that "the small powers should be given an adequate role to play in any arrangement which concerned the peace and security of the world."[1] The Indian delegation

[1] Swadesh Mehta, "The Organization of an International Force," *International Studies* (New Delhi), Vol. VII, No. 2 (October 1965), p. 207.

believed that the small powers had a part to play in the maintenance of peace. It maintained that "the smaller nations who have contributed a little one way or the other may also in times of stress be not altogether a negligible factor in maintaining security."[2]

India was favorably inclined toward Secretary-General Trygvie Lie's proposals to establish a force by the United Nations to protect its missions. The proposal to establish a United Nations Guard received sympathetic consideration from India. Mr. H. S. Malik felt that the proposal should be examined thoroughly and stated that "it was of great importance that it should be possible to place complete confidence in the independence and integrity of the Guard."[3] To maintain the international character of the Guard, he desired that the recruitment of the Guard be based on "wide and fair geographical distribution."[4] India showed a greater interest in Mr. Lie's proposal to establish a United Nations Field Service to provide United Nations missions with the technical services necessary for their smooth operation and for ensuring the protection of the staff of those missions. Sir B. N. Rau stated that "there could be no doubt that the Field Service, which would involve only modest expenditures, would contribute greatly to the success of United Nations missions."[5] He emphasized that the Field Service "should be used only in cases where, owing to circumstances beyond their control, the local authorities could not give the missions the necessary protection and technical services; that

[2] UNCIO 11 (Documents 956, 489), Quoted in Swadesh Mehta, op. cit., p. 207.

[3] United Nations, General Assembly, Third Session, Part 11, Official Records, Ad Hoc Political Committee, 32nd meeting (11 April 1949) (Lake Success, 1950), p. 41.

[4] Ibid.

[5] United Nations, General Assembly, Fourth Session, Official Records, Ad Hoc Political Committee, 2nd meeting (26 October 1949) (New York, 1950), p. 108.

was essential in order to avoid any superfluous expenditure and any friction with the authorities of the countries concerned."[6]

INDIA'S VIEW OF THE UNITED NATIONS
AS AN ENFORCEMENT AGENCY

While India was willing to support proposals for establishing a small force to protect United Nations missions, she was opposed to making the United Nations an enforcement agency in the absence of great power unanimity. In the maintenance of peace and security through enforcement action, India advocated adherence to the provisions of the Charter. Indian delegates insisted that only the Security Council could take enforcement action in accordance with Article 39 of the Charter and for such action great power unanimity was required.[7] They looked with disdain upon Western attempts to provide armed forces for the United Nations through the "Uniting for Peace Resolution." India was against Sections C and D of the Resolution which required Member-States to maintain armed units for service with the United Nations upon requisition by the Security Council or the General Assembly. The Government of India opposed the creation of an international army and refused to earmark any of its forces for a stand-by United Nations force.[8] Indians feared that the Assembly, as it was then constituted, might attempt enforcement action against a great

[6] *Ibid.* Like Mr. Malik, he felt that the Field Service, to be really international, should be recruited on the basis of "the widest possible geographical distribution." *Ibid.*

[7] United Nations, General Assembly, Ninth Session, *Official Records,* First Committee, 706th meeting, agenda item 19 (2 November 1954) (New York, 1955), p. 288.

[8] *Facts on File Yearbook 1951,* Vol. 11, No. 565 (August 24-31, 1951), p. 275 H.

power which would result in serious repercussions. According to Karunakaran "it was feared in India that the forces earmarked by member states for use by the UN would not be at the disposal of the UN but at the disposal of the dominant bloc (in the Assembly). If this happened, it would mean the death of the UN as an instrument of peaceful settlement of disputes and the emergence in its place of a global military alliance directed against a group of powers headed by the Soviet Union."[9]

Mr. Nehru thought that the United Nations had the right to use military force whenever and wherever needed. However, the use of the United Nations as an enforcement agency in the presence of Soviet objections would not lead to peace. Pointing to Western attempts to set up a United Nations force on the basis of the Uniting for Peace Resolution, he held the view that under the prevalent situation an international force was unnecessary. He argued that it was not likely to produce any effective result but was likely to produce a certain atmosphere and a psychology of war and fear.[10] Mr. Nehru stated that the United Nations could take a police or military action on a small scale but it could not take sanctions against very powerful nations without having a world war.[11] India was apprehensive that the implementation of the Uniting for Peace Resolution could result in such an eventuality.

Mr. Malik reiterated Nehru's views at the United Nations and said that the responsibility to determine a threat to or a breach of the peace was placed on the Security Council and

[9] Karunakaran, *India in World Affairs 1950-53, op. cit.,* p. 136. See also I.C.W.A. Study, *op. cit.,* p. 144, and Varma, "India's Policy in the United Nations with Respect to the Maintenance of Peace and Security," *op. cit.,* p. 91.

[10] *Special Press Release* (Washington, D. C.: Government of India Information Services, date not specified), p. 3.

[11] *Ibid.*

it was for the Council to determine the appropriate measures for maintaining peace.[12]

India was skeptical of achieving the maintenance of peace and security by perfecting the United Nations enforcement machinery. According to a study group of the Indian Council of World Affairs "it was feared in India that perfecting the United Nations machinery for the purpose of war might itself lead to a major armed conflict in the world."[13] In the same vein Mr. Malik contended that Western efforts to perfect the United Nations enforcement machinery would only increase tension and ill will in the world. He stated that "the world looks to the United Nations for relief from this tension and for it to take steps toward the attainment of peace, and in our opinion it is very important that the emphasis on our work here should at the present time be on measures which would promote the whole conception of conciliation and mediation."[14] Commenting on the report of the Collective Measures Committee which dealt with the implementing of the Uniting for Peace Resolution, Mr. Malik brusquely remarked that "at a time when the world hoped for a reduction of tension, the Indian delegation considered it inopportune for the United Nations to adopt a proposal that might increase mutual suspicions."[15] While

[12] United Nations, General Assembly, Sixth Session, *Official Records,* 359th plenary meeting, agenda item 18 (12 January 1952) (Paris, 1953), p. 326. It was considered that enforcement action without the concurrence of the big powers was a dangerous step for the United Nations to take. See I.C.W.A. Study, *op. cit.,* p. 54.

[13] I.C.W.A. Study, *op. cit.,* p. 209.

[14] United Nations, General Assembly, Sixth Session, *Official Records,* 359th plenary meeting, agenda item 18 (12 January 1951) (Paris, 1952), p. 326. He felt that provisions relating to collective measures in the Uniting for Peace Resolution would put undue emphasis upon the enforcement machinery rather than upon the possibilities of cooperation offered by the United Nations. *Ibid.*

[15] United Nations, General Assembly, Sixth Session, *Official Records,* First Committee, 483rd meeting, item 18 (7 January 1952) (Paris, 1952), p. 155.

India was reluctant to support proposals to strengthen the coercive aspect of the United Nations, she repeatedly stressed the cooperative character of the United Nations. Madame Pandit maintained that the United Nations, instead of placing emphasis on coercive measures, should devote itself to a study of measures for the peaceful settlement and conciliation of disputes. She held that the need for such a study was "more urgent and more constructive than the study of coercive measures."[16]

INDIA AND THE UNITED NATIONS EMERGENCY FORCE

The Secretary-General's request for Indian troops to join the United Nations Emergency Force (UNEF) gave India a great opportunity to largely define and determine the role of the force. On his arrival in New York in November 1956, Mr. Krishna Menon took upon himself the task of interpreting the functions and powers of the UNEF. He not only set out several terms for India's participation in the UNEF but also utilized the occasion to interpret the intentions of the Secretary-General about the role of the UNEF. He elaborated by pointing out that "the emergency force would be set up in the context of the withdrawal of the Franco-British forces from Egypt and on the basis of the call to Israel to withdraw behind the armistice lines; secondly, that that Force would not in any sense be a successor to the invading Franco-British forces, or would in any sense take over its functions; thirdly, that it would be understood that the Force might have to function through Egyptian territory and, therefore, that the Egyptian Government must consent

[16] United Nations, General Assembly, Seventh Session, *Official Records*, First Committee, 575th meeting, item 18 (16 March 1953) (New York, 1953), p. 454.

to its establishment; fourthly, that the Force would be a temporary one for the emergency. . . . The Force must be of a balanced composition."[17] Mr. Menon repeatedly emphasized that the UNEF was not an army of invasion and with regard to the length of its stay in Egypt, he said that "the forces would arrive only with Egypt's consent, and that they could not stay or operate unless Egypt continued to give such consent."[18] He did not favor an enlargement of the functions of the UNEF and contended that such an enlargement would require basic consideration, consultation and agreement by all the parties concerned. Pointing to the risks and dangers involved in widening the responsibilities of the UNEF, Mr. Menon warned that "already we have a situation where an army is functioning without any restraint from a legislature or a government, and we ourselves would not want to find ourselves in a position where this army would be assuming responsibilities involving the use of lethal weapons without the previous commitment of our governments."[19] Thus Mr. Menon wished that the governments should retain control over the functioning of the UNEF. India wanted Member-States to determine the formation as well as the opera-

---

[17] United Nations, General Assembly, First Emergency Special Session, *Official Records,* 567th plenary meeting, agenda item 5 (7 November 1956) (New York, 1957), p. 117. The Secretary-General concurred with Mr. Menon's interpretation and said that Mr. Menon's interpretation of the former's intentions was correct. *Ibid.,* p. 119.

[18] United Nations, General Assembly, Eleventh Session, *Official Records,* Vol. 1, 596th plenary meeting, agenda item 66 (2 November 1956) (New York, 1957), p. 333. For Mr. Menon's reiteration of these views see *Ibid.,* 594th meeting (24 November 1956), p. 305; and *Ibid.,* Vol. 2, 651st plentary meeting (2 February 1957), p. 1071.

[19] United Nations, General Assembly, Eleventh Session, *Official Records,* 641st plenary meeting, agenda item 66 (18 January 1957) (New York, 1957), p. 930. In his view the functions of the UNEF were the obtaining of a cease fire and the supervision of the withdrawal of non-Egyptian forces from Egypt. See *Ibid.,* Vol. 2, 665 plenary meeting (1 March 1957), p. 1268.

tion of the Force, keeping to themselves the power to expand or contract its role.

Although India did not favor an enlargement of the functions of the UNEF, Indian leaders recognized that the Force had proved useful by stopping the fighting and by keeping peace in the Middle East. Mr. G. S. Pathak of the Indian delegation expressed satisfaction at the way in which the Force was functioning and thought that it should continue its functions.[20] Mr. Menon referred to India's participation in the UNEF and its role in maintaining peace in Gaza and said that India and the Scandinavian countries were doing something which was very much in furtherance of the Charter.[21] India desired that every assistance should be given to the UNEF to overcome any difficulties that might arise. In the view of the Indian delegation "the United Nations was making a great experiment in creating the Force, and nothing should be done that might discourage the formation of a similar force if it became necessary in the future."[22] India provided valuable assistance in organizing the UNEF by persuading Egypt to accept Canadian troops and helped its functioning by contributing a substantial number of contingents to it.[23]

[20] United Nations, General Assembly, Thirteenth Session, *Official Records,* Special Political Committee, 97th meeting, agenda item 65 (29 October 1958) (New York, 1959), p. 51. In 1963 Mr. S. K. Singh expressing the same view said that the UNEF had "helped to safeguard peace and had made any new crisis unlikely." See United Nations, General Assembly, Eighteenth Session, *Official Records,* Fifth Committee, agenda item 19 (13 December 1963) (New York, 1964), p. 287.

[21] United Nations, General Assembly, Twelfth Session, *Official Records,* 703rd plenary meeting, agenda item 9 (8 October 1957) (New York, 1958), p. 324.

[22] United Nations, General Assembly, Eleventh Session, *Official Records,* Fifth Committee, 541st meeting, agenda item 66 (3 December 1956) (New York, 1957), p. 43.

[23] William R. Frye, *A United Nations Peace Force* (New York: Oceana Publications Inc., 1957), pp. 29-30. As of May, 1966 India has an infantry batallion of about 1,000 soldiers serving with the UNEF.

INDIA AND THE UNITED NATIONS FORCE IN THE CONGO

Although India held many reservations about the establishment of a permanent United Nations force, India's desire to restore peace prompted her to take part in the United Nations peace-keeping operations. India contributed contingents and enthusiastically participated in the United Nations Force in the Congo (ONUC). India advocated vigorous and strong action, including the use of force, by the ONUC for achieving the United Nations purposes in the Congo. Mr. Krishna Menon was critical of the Secretary-General's hesitation to instruct the ONUC to use force for maintaining law and order, civil liberties and the integrity of the Congo. Questioning the Secretary-General's interpretation that the United Nations troops could use force only in self-defense, Mr. Menon argued that "if there was no question of using force, why did the Security Council, in its first resolution on July 14, 1960, take steps to send 20,000 armed troops to the Congo? They were not going to play in a tournament. If the idea was not to use force, then engineers, scientists, parsons and preachers would have gone."[24] While criticizing inaction of the United Nations and its reluctance to employ force, India indicated her readiness to contribute combat troops if the United Nations were to follow a more vigorous and effective policy in the Congo. Mr. C. S. Jha expressed India's willingness to make whatever further contribution India could, to the success of the United Nations operation in the Congo.[25] Mr. Nehru offered to provide com-

[24] United Nations, General Assembly, Fifteenth Session, Part 1, *Official Records,* Vol. 2, 957th plenary meeting, agenda item 85 (19 December 1960) (New York, 1961), p. 1455.

[25] United Nations, Security Council, *Official Records,* 941st meeting (20 February 1961) (New York, 1961), p. 11.

bat troops to the ONUC if it was really necessary from the point of view of the world and of the Congo[26] on the condition that the Indian forces would be used rightly.[27] When the Security Council authorized the ONUC to use force in the Congo, Mr. Nehru made it clear that he supported such authorization[28] and voiced his approval for the continuation of the Congo operation.[29]

The request of the Secretary-General for Indian combat troops provided India an opportunity to set out certain terms for India's participation in the ONUC. India utilized the occasion to present her views more forcefully than before. While contributing troops, Indian leaders proceeded to lay down conditions determining the functions and powers of the ONUC. While Indian leaders expressed eagerness to participate in the ONUC, they were equally anxious to set limits to its role. The Government of India informed the Secretary-General that they did not wish Indian forces to fight troops or nationals of other Member-States, apart from the Congolese armed units and Belgian and other military and para-military personnel, and other mercenaries. The Indian Government also stated that they "did not wish Indian armed forces to be used for the suppression of popular movements or in any way in support of parties or factions that were challenging United Nations authority. Nor did the Indian Government wish that the (Indian) brigade should be broken up and mixed with other armed contingents, but that at command level it would remain under its own officers."[30]

---

[26] Nehru, *India's Foreign Policy, op. cit.,* pp. 524-525.

[27] *Facts on File Yearbook 1961,* Vol. XXI, No. 1060 (February 16-22, 1961), p. 61D[2]. See also *Ibid.,* No. 1062 (March 2-8, 1961), p. 77F[3].

[28] *Ibid.,* No. 1061 (February 23-March 1, 1961), p. 71D[1].

[29] *The New York Times,* February 28, 1961, p. 1.

[30] "Reports on the Congo: Implementation of Council Resolution and Further Exchanges of Message," *United Nations Review,* Vol. 8, No. 4

Indian leaders persisted with their demand for decisive action by the United Nations in the Congo. Mr. Nehru insisted that the United Nations should function in the Congo even if it was necessary to use armed force and not merely to look on while others used force for a wrong purpose.[31] When the United Nations took decisive steps in the Congo, Mr. Krishna Menon defended the projection of military might by the United Nations as necessary and supported the ONUC's taking over of military bases from the Congolese forces. He argued that the United Nations troops were entitled to the use of military bases and if that use was denied, then there was a breach of the agreement entered into by the United Nations with the Republic of the Congo. He contended that the United Nations operation in the Congo was not in violation of the sovereignty of the Congo and it would be wrong to think that the United Nations was a kind of imperial power that was trying to protect itself.[32] In 1963, Mr. B. C. Chakravarty stated that India favored the continuation of an effective force if that would help to ease the problems of the Congolese Government. He claimed that India made far more than a mere token contribution for ONUC and said that "India was anxious that the gains al-

---

(April, 1961), p. 13. India recognized the United Nations authority over the national contingents in the ONUC. Mr. Menon stated that the national contingents under the United Nations were the international forces of the world and their movements and use would be regulated by the command of the Secretary-General, subject to the agreement that the United Nations reached with the participating states. See United Nations, General Assembly, Fifteenth Session, Part 11, *Official Records,* 977th plenary meeting, agenda item 85 (5 April 1961) (New York, 1961), p. 205. See also United Nations, General Assembly, Sixteenth Session, *Official Records,* Vol. 1, 1025th plenary meeting, agenda item 9 (4 October 1961) (New York, 1962), p. 249.

[31] Nehru, *India's Foreign Policy, op. cit.,* p. 526.

[32] United Nations, General Assembly, Fifteenth Session, Part 11, *Official Records,* 977th plenary meeting, agenda item 85 (5 April 1961) (New York, 1961), p. 198.

ready made in the Congo should not be jeopardized by a premature withdrawal of the United Nations force."[33]

ATTITUDE TOWARD THE ESTABLISHMENT OF
A PERMANENT PEACE FORCE

India exhibited extreme disinclination toward proposals to establish a permanent United Nations force. At the Twelfth Session Mr. Krishna Menon discouraged those who entertained the idea of making the UNEF a pilot project or an embryonic international force of the future. He made it clear that India would not subscribe to such a view. He explained that it was a problem by itself and some development could come about when the great powers had resolved their problems among themselves. He stated that the UNEF was conceived and improvised for a specific purpose. He argued that it was not working according to the plan of the Charter and contended that the Force was not responsible to the Security Council and it was difficult to say to whom it was responsible.[34] The Indian delegation maintained in 1965 that it was now recognized that all enforcement actions or actions of coercive nature were the prerogative of the Security Council. An Indian delegate at the United Nations observed that it was generally agreed that even action which fell short of enforcement was primarily the responsibility of the Security Council. He thought that "it might be practical to reach an

[33] United Nations, General Assembly, Eighteenth Session, *Official Records,* Fifth Committee, 1015th meeting, agenda item 59 (10 October 1963) (New York, 1964), p. 44. The 1962 Indian reverses on her northern border did not prompt the Government of India to make a hasty withdrawal of Indian troops from the ONUC.

[34] United Nations, General Assembly, Twelfth Session, *Official Records,* 703rd plenary meeting, agenda item 9 (8 October 1957) (New York, 1958), p. 324. Mr. G. S. Pathak also maintained that the UNEF was a special force set up to meet a specific situation and that no general conclusions could be drawn from that one experience. See United Nations, General Assembly, Thirteenth Session, *Official Records,* Special Political Committee, 97th meeting, agenda item 65 (29 October 1958) (New York, 1959), p. 51.

agreement that the dispatch of armed personnel for reasons other than the mere observation or investigation should be within the exclusive power of the Security Council."[35] Madame Pandit expressed the view that unless the great powers decide to establish the force envisaged in the Charter, the United Nations should rely on ad hoc forces raised to meet each situation.[36]

Mr. Krishna Menon reiterated India's opposition to the establishment of a permanent United Nations force. In 1958, he stated that India was "irrevocably opposed to the conception of the creation of an international police force unless the world disarms."[37] In his view the suggestion for the establishment of such a force was an impractical proposition. He explained India's objections to the setting up of a permanent force in detail. He stated: "It is not possible for any country to put by a certain number of soldiers and officers and say: 'You are there to go out when there is trouble in the world.' First of all what do they do when there is no trouble in the world? ... Secondly, if they were so kept and did not participate in the general military organization of the country, they would be no longer competent to perform the task for which they were sent out. Over and above that, which country is to be selected for this purpose? One country may be acceptable in one situation; the same country may not be acceptable in another situation."[38]

[35] "Peace-Keeping Operations: Committee Hears Statements," *United Nations Monthly Chronicle,* Vol. 11, No. 11 (December, 1965), p. 73.
[36] "Assembly Calls for New Disarmament Talks," *United Nations Review,* Vol. 11, No. 1 (January, 1964), p. 23. See also Mehta, *op. cit.,* p. 221.
[37] United Nations, General Assembly, Thirteenth Session, *Official Records,* 774th plenary meeting, agenda item 9 (7 October 1958) (New York, 1959), p. 365. See also *The New York Times,* October 7, 1959, p. 17.
[38] *Ibid.* In 1959 Mr. Menon again stated that "the Government of India is not at present prepared to participate in a standing force of the United Nations" because, in his view, it was not a practical proposition to have troops demarcated in the defense force of any country for service with the United Nations. See United Nations, General Assembly, Four-

India was apprehensive that the United Nations might decide to dispatch an international force, if a permanent United Nations force were to be in existence, into a state without the consent of that state. Indian representatives repeatedly emphasized that the consent of a state, in which United Nations force was to be stationed, was essential. Mr. Menon maintained that India "could not consent to the taking of troops to the soil of the countries, even though they are United Nations troops, for they are still foreign troops."[39] While agreeing to join the UNEF, India stressed, as earlier noted, that Egypt's consent was a prerequisite for the introduction of United Nations force into Gaza. The Government of India made it clear that India's active participation in UNEF could "only be decided after seeing the final plan which must have the consent of the Egyptian Government."[40] Mr. Menon maintained a similar position with regard to Hungary and opposed the idea of the United Nations sending observers to Hungary without first ascertaining the consent of the Hungarian Government.[41]

India's insistence on Egypt's prior approval for the sta-

---

teenth Session, Part 1, *Official Records*, Vol. 1, 823rd plenary meeting, agenda item 9 (6 October 1959) (New York, 1960), p. 215. According to Swadesh Mehta the absence of great-power agreement for a permanent international force, the impracticality, the perennial nature of its composition, the risks involved in having an international force with national backgrounds, the possibility that it might not be needed all the time, the cost, the dependence of its effectiveness on the consent of the state where the force was to operate and the Indian belief that the time was not yet ripe for its setup were some of the reasons for India's objection to the establishment of a permanent United Nations Force. See Swadesh Mehta, *op. cit.*, pp. 215-221.

[39] *Ibid.*

[40] Quoted in James G. Eayers *The Commonwealth and Suez, A Documentary Survey* (London: Oxford University Press, 1964), p. 361. The Indian Government stated that the invitation for India to join the UNEF was supported by Egypt. *Ibid.*

[41] United Nations, General Assembly, Eleventh Session, *Official Records,* Vol. 1, 586th plenary meeting, agenda item 67 (21 November 1956) (New York, 1957), p. 168.

tioning of United Nations forces and on Hungary's consent for the dispatch of United Nations observers seemed to have stemmed from her desire to safeguard her position over Kashmir. Indians repeatedly rejected proposals to station United Nations forces in Kashmir. In 1957, Mr. Krishna Menon bluntly told the Security Council that the Council "dare not" ask India to accept the introduction of foreign troops in Kashmir and added that India would reject any attempt to introduce war elements even under the banner of the United Nations.[42] In 1965, Mr. Lal Bahadur Shastri informed the Secretary-General that there could be no peace-keeping force on Indian territory.[43] India's anxiety to prevent the introduction of an international force into Kashmir led her to dramatize the factor of consent. India's insistence on the prior acceptance of the state concerned to the entry of United Nations force stemmed from her desire to safeguard her position over Kashmir. When Pakistan proposed in 1965 to dispatch a United Nations force to Kashmir, the Indian delegate pointed out that "let it be clear beyond any doubt that nowhere have Indian troops been sent without the consent of the governments concerned."[44]

[42] "The Kashmir Question: Security Council Again Calls for a Plebiscite." *United Nations Review,* Vol. 3, No. 9 (March, 1957), p. 13.

[43] *The Times,* London, September 28, 1965, p. 10. To Mr. Swaran Singh the proposal to send a United Nations force to Kashmir was totally unacceptable. See *The Hindu Weekly Review,* October 4, 1965, p. 3.

[44] "General debate: Summaries of Statements made at Twentieth Session of General Assembly," *UN Monthly Chronicle,* Vol. 11, No. 9 (October, 1965), p. 67. It was this Indian objective to protect her interests in Kashmir that prompted India to insist on so many reservations for her participation in the UNEF. According to Eayers India viewed the project of resorting to an international force, during the Suez crisis, with the greatest suspicion and held the most reservations. India desired to guard herself from establishing a precedent in taking collective measures lest they threaten the Indian position over Kashmir. See Eayers, p. 294. Mr. Frye attributed India's opposition to the establishment of a permanent peace force to Indian susceptibilities over Kashmir. See Frye, *op. cit.,* pp. 37-38.

The suggestions for establishing a United Nations force on a permanent basis were repugnant to Mr. Krishna Menon. He warned that the very idea of setting up of a permanent force whose authority and power of sanctions was questionable, was fraught with danger and said that it would endanger the position of small states. Mr. Menon, explaining his apprehensions, pointed out to the delegates that "we must think hard and see that we do not get a situation where the United Nations, as at present composed, becomes a kind of superstate with its representatives directing governments, which is not provided for in the Charter, and where the Secretary-General will be pushed away from his Charter functions into other matters. . . . we have to see that we do not exceed the cautious balances that have been introduced into the Charter for the preservation of national sovereignty and for the preservation of small nations. If this rather superior power should be at the disposal of a snap vote of a two-thirds majority, the position of small states and minorities would be far from enviable."[45] India's belief in the existence of an imbalance in the General Assembly and her fear that the dominant group might employ a permanent force to the disadvantage of a small state influenced India's opposition to the establishment of a permanent force. Mr. Menon thought that groups existed in the United Nations and felt that it was risky to place a permanent force in the hands of such an organization. He stated that "we as an organization are far from free from group politics or yet capable of taking truly objective decisions; we do not think that it would be right to place at the disposal of such an Organization forces which may be moved in without individual nego-

[45] United Nations, General Assembly, Thirteenth Session, *Official Records,* 774th plenary meeting, agenda item 9 (7 October 1958) (New York, 1959), p. 365.

tiations and the consent of the people concerned."[46] Mr. Swaran Singh also held that the United Nations could form a force only by negotiating agreements with the contributing states and contended that no member state could be compelled to contribute either troops or funds to the United Nations peace-keeping operations.[47] He categorically stated that India was not in favor of setting apart certain military contingents for service with the United Nations.[48]

India questioned the views that a standardized permanent international force could meet all types of situations. Mr. Arthur S. Lall stated that the United Nations Truce Supervision Organization in Palestine, the UNEF and the United Nations Observation Group in Lebanon were "so different one from another, that no single force could answer to all these widely differing requirements. To rush a standard type of force into delicate situations which cannot possibly be standardized is to court added trouble and disaster."[49] He maintained that a chameleon-like force, capable of changing its color or character, to meet all kinds of requirements, could not be created.

Although India was disinclined to support proposals for

[46] United Nations, General Assembly, Fourteenth Session, Part 1, *Official Records,* Vol. 1, 823rd plenary meeting, agenda item 9 (6 October 1959) (New York, 1960), p. 416. In Mr. Menon's view it was premature to speak in terms of a United Nations force or to expect countries to shoulder the responsibility from the point of view of personnel, money and political acceptances. *Ibid.*

[47] United Nations, General Assembly, Nineteenth Session, *Official Records,* Vol. 11, 1301st plenary meeting, item 9 of the provisional agenda (14 December 1964) (New York, 1966), p. 11.

[48] *Ibid.,* p. 12. In 1963 India did not join the Scandinavian countries in offering to the Secretary-General special "stand-by" military units for use in the United Nations peace-keeping operations. See " 'Stand-by' Military Units," *United Nations Review,* Vol. 10, No. 11 (November, 1963), p. 1.

[49] United Nations, General Assembly, Third Emergency Special Session, *Official Records,* 738th plenary meeting, agenda item 5 (18 August 1958) (New York, 1958), p. 69.

the establishment of a permanent United Nations force, she was willing to support a study of the various peace-keeping operations. Mr. Menon was of the view that the experience gained in Korea, Gaza and Lebanon should be studied and kept for future reference.[50] Mr. Swaran Singh displayed the same disposition by observing that India had no objection "to a study which might lead to 'more efficient and more economical peace-keeping operations in the future.' "[51] Indian spokesmen recognized the need for a study of the peace-keeping operations for improving such operations in the future. In 1963, Madame Pandit said that India was aware that the peace-keeping operations were closely linked with problems of political control, executive direction, financial means and administrative coordination, and suggested that the Disarmament Committee should consider methods to organize a force capable of maintaining peace.

India's contribution in shaping the nature of peace-keeping forces could largely be attributed to the lack of consensus among the permanent members of the Security Council for establishing an enforcement agency. Another factor was the occurrence of serious crises affecting international peace and security. By setting conditions for India's participation, by contributing large numbers of forces and considerable amounts of military supplies India successfully attempted to bring the peace-keeping operations more in line with her own views. The United Nations request from time to time for Indian troops satisfied India's desire for recogni-

[50] United Nations, General Assembly, Thirteenth Session, *Official Records,* 774th plenary meeting, agenda item 9 (7 October 1958) (New York, 1959), p. 365.

[51] *Ibid.,* 1301st plenary meeting, item 9 of the provisional agenda (14 December 1964) (New York, 1964), p. 12. India participated in the 1964 Ottawa Conference on the Techniques of UN Peace-Keeping which was held to discuss the technical aspects of United Nations peace-keeping forces and to consider methods of improving the efficiency of such forces.

tion in world affairs. India utilized every opportunity to contribute either troops or officers or both and thus participated actively in the United Nations peace-keeping operations. India's sensitivity over Kashmir was largely responsible for India's insistence on many conditions, reservations and interpretations about the functioning of United Nations forces. Indians believed in the existence of snatch majorities and snap votes in the General Assembly and feared the possibilities of the dominant group employing a permanent force against a great power or small states. This feeling was also responsible for India's setting up of so many terms whenever the United Nations undertook peace-keeping operations.

Although the imbalance in the United Nations General Assembly had become, with the increase in the Organization's membership, a thing of the past, India would still prefer to leave enforcement action to the Security Council. While India's opposition to the establishment of a permanent force by the General Assembly stemmed from a desire to adhere to the Charter provisions over enforcement machinery, her resistance also would seem to have arisen from her desire to have a voice in the United Nations peace-keeping operations. India's influence in determining the role and functions of an ad hoc peace force in each situation would be greater than her ability to influence the activities of a permanent force. India would naturally prefer an ad hoc force over a permanent one because she could keep a finger on the trigger and could retain the right to provide or to refuse troops to such a force. It is very likely India will continue to support United Nations peace-keeping operations in situations where great powers are not directly involved. She will invariably oppose the use of a United Nations force against a great power.

5

India's Policy Toward Financing the United Nations

INDIA'S ADVOCACY OF THE PRINCIPLE OF CAPACITY TO PAY

India insisted that the principle of capacity to pay should be applied by the United Nations in assessing contributions from member states. India felt that the assessment on her did not correspond to her capacity to pay. Indian delegates persistently demanded a reduction in India's contribution. Mr. D. P. Adarkar stated that "the principle of capacity to pay was of fundamental importance"[1] and contended that "the contribution required of India was out of all proportion to its

[1] United Nations, General Assembly, Sixth Session, *Official Records,* Fifth Committee, 307th meeting, item 4 (10 December 1951) (Paris, 1952), p. 132.

capacity to pay."[2] In 1950, Nawab Ali Yawar Jung felt that the assessments drawn by the Committee on Contributions continue to be inequitable and complained that in assessing India's contribution the Committee had not taken into consideration such factors as India's economic instability and inadequate foreign exchange reserves. He favored the continuation of the existing scale of assessments and insisted that a higher assessment should not be placed on India.[3]

While calling for a reduction in India's contribution, the Indian delegates contended that the United States and other developed nations should bear a large proportion of the United Nations expenses. Jam Sahib of Nawanagar, an Indian delegate at the Third Session, while considering the report of the Committee on Contributions, appealed to the United States "to postpone the application of a ceiling on contributions until normal conditions returned."[4] At the Sixth Session, Mr. Adarkar opposed an increase in India's contribution; at the same time he insisted that the United States contribution should not be reduced. He stated that "each year the assessment of India, like that of other countries, had been unjustifiably increased and if the same principles were applied in the future, there was every indication that the burden would continue to grow, that the United States assessment would be steadily reduced and that the resultant burden would be borne by countries with an average and very low per capita income."[5] He believed that the

[2] *Ibid.,* p. 133.

[3] United Nations, General Assembly, Fifth Session, *Official Records,* Fifth Committee, 273rd meeting, item 40 (30 November 1950) (Lake Success, 1951), p. 236.

[4] United Nations, General Assembly, Third Session, Part I, *Official Records,* Fifth Committee, 112th meeting (30 September 1948) (Paris, 1949), p. 85.

[5] United Nations, General Assembly, Sixth Session, *Official Records,* Fifth Committee, 307th meeting, item 4 (10 December 1951) (Paris, 1952), p. 132. In 1956 Mr. R. Venkataraman expressed the same view and said that any reduction in the United States contribution would

constant rise in the United Nations expenditures would also lead to an increase in the amount of contributions of the poorer countries.

Referring to the United States demand for a reduction in the American contribution, Mr. Adarkar argued that the contribution of the United States should actually be increased since her capacity to pay was steadily increasing.[6] He held the view that in contributing finances to the United Nations the richer countries of North America and Western Europe "could unquestionably afford to be more generous than the underdeveloped countries."[7] When the Committee on Contributions proposed in 1951 a reduction in the contributions of developed nations, Mr. Adarkar contended that the proposed reduction in the assessments of European countries was unfair because of the fact that economic progress in certain European countries had been very rapid while the underdeveloped countries had made very slow progress.[8]

Mr. Adarkar attempted to show that although the United States contributed a high percentage of the United Nations expenditure, the net contribution of the United States was far below its assessment figure. He pointed out that the United States, though not benefiting economically from the United Nations, was still deriving income from the activities of the Organization. He stated that to obtain a balanced picture of the United States financial contribution to the regular budget of the United Nations, "account should also be taken of the outlay on the permanent delegations in New York.

---

result in an increase in the contributions of other countries, causing repercussions to countries with a low per-capita income. See United Nations, General Assembly, Eleventh Session, *Official Records,* Fifth Committee, 538th meeting, agenda item 46 (27 November 1956) (New York, 1957), p. 28.

[6] *Ibid.,* p. 133.

[7] *Ibid.*

[8] *Ibid.*

Again staff members who were nationals of the United States paid United States taxes which were reimbursed by the Organization. In actual fact, therefore, the net cost to the United States did not exceed, perhaps, fifteen percent."[9] In 1953 Mr. Azim Husain, a member of the Indian delegation at the Eighth Session, held that the United States contribution figure had been reduced to 33.33 per cent through the payment to the United States Treasury of the income tax of the United States citizens in the United Nations staff.[10]

India considered that the United Nations requirement that contributions should be paid in United States dollars was a heavy burden to the developing states. For easing the financial difficulties of developing countries, Indian delegates favored the payment of contributions to the United Nations budget in currencies other than the United States dollar. In 1948, the Jam Sahib of Nawanagar hoped that "arrangements might be made for payments whenever possible in soft currencies."[11] Nawab Ali Yawar Jung thought that an increase in the expenditure of the United Nations in soft currencies would make it possible for countries to make contributions in soft currencies. Considering the report of the Committee on Contributions in 1951, he "emphasized the

[9] *Ibid.* Replying to the United States delegate, he contended that the large sums paid by the United States for various United Nations programs were purely voluntary contributions, affecting in no way the obligatory contributions to the regular budget. Mr. Venkataraman also maintained in 1956 that most of the United Nations funds were spent in the United States and that the money spent by delegations and visitors was in the nature of invisible revenue, occurring to the United States. See United Nations, General Assembly, Eleventh Session, *Official Records,* Fifth Committee, 538th meeting, agenda item 46 (27 November 1956) (New York, 1957), p. 28.

[10] United Nations, General Assembly, Eighth Session, *Official Records,* Fifth Committee, 395th meeting, item 42 (22 October 1953) (New York, 1954), p. 101.

[11] United Nations, General Assembly, Third Session, Part I, *Official Records,* Fifth Committee, 106th meeting (27 September 1948) (Paris, 1949), p. 16.

great need for the United Nations to place more orders in soft currency countries under such heads as travel, printing, stores and equipment."[12] Pointing to the increasing use of soft currencies by the United Nations, Mr. Adarkar insisted in 1951 that the United Nations should make more frequent use of soft currencies by making a greater proportion of its purchases in countries outside the hard currency area and by paying salaries to its personnel stationed in those countries in soft currencies.[13]

India's insistence on the acceptance of payments in non-dollar currencies was due to her "difficulties in finding the requisite amount of foreign exchange."[14] In 1963, Mr. B. N. Chakravarty pointed to the difficulties of the developing nations in meeting the increasing expenses of the United Nations and said that the United Nations should welcome payments in currencies other than the United States dollars.[15] He thought that the United Nations could usefully utilize the soft currencies in carrying out the various technical assistance programs in the developing countries.

[12] United Nations, General Assembly, Fifth Session, *Official Records,* Fifth Committee, 273rd meeting, item 40 (30 November 1950) (Lake Success, 1951), p. 236.

[13] United Nations, General Assembly, Sixth Session, *Official Records,* Fifth Committee, 313th meeting, item 28 (14 December 1951) (Paris, 1952), p. 168. In 1953 Mr. Azim Husain reiterated India's hope that means would be sought to increase still further the portion paid in soft currencies and that the difficult position of the underdeveloped countries would be kept in mind in assessing contributions. See United Nations, General Assembly, Eighth Session, *Official Records,* Fifth Committee, 395th meeting, item 42 (22 October 1953) (New York, 1954), p. 101.

[14] United Nations, General Assembly, Eleventh Session, *Official Records,* Fifth Committee, 609th meeting, item 41 (22 October 1957) (New York, 1957), p. 46. While India had difficulties in obtaining United States dollars, she had a large proportion of her foreign exchange reserves in pound sterling and wanted to pay her contribution, if not in Indian currency, at least in pound sterling.

[15] United Nations, General Assembly, Eighteenth Session, *Official Records,* 1015th meeting, agenda item 59 (10 October 1963) (New York, 1965), p. 113.

FINANCING ECONOMIC DEVELOPMENT

Generally India did not favor increases in the expenditures of the United Nations. While India desired to keep the United Nations budget at as low a level as possible, she urged the approval of the budget estimates of the Secretariat for economic development. India's opposition to increases in the United Nations expenses stemmed from her fear that they would become a burden on the developing countries. India's desire to benefit from the economic projects of the United Nations led her to advocate the retention of the estimates on developmental schemes. Favoring a reduction in the expenditure of the United Nations, Mr. Jung stated in 1950 that "economies were necessary to avoid any increase in the contributions which fell particularly heavily on the soft currency countries."[16] But during the Sixth Session, Mr. Adarkar contended that the United Nations had to incur considerable expenses because numerous problems existed in the world and because many areas in the world were suffering from want, disease, sickness and fear. Expressing India's opposition to any excessive reduction in the budget estimates on developmental programs, he stated that "economy was not synonymous with parsimony or avarice. The (Fifth) Committee should carefully consider the estimated expenditure and prune it as far as possible, while, however, avoiding the arbitrary restriction of useful and desirable international activities. His delegation was keenly interested in the efforts of the United Nations in the economic and social fields, including technical assistance to underdeveloped countries. India was situated in a region which, being one of the poorest

[16] United Nations, General Assembly, Fifth Session, *Official Records,* Fifth Committee, 239th meeting, item 39 (3 October 1950) (Lake Success, 1951), p. 17.

in the world, also stood in the greatest need, and his delegation would unhesitatingly oppose any arbitrary reduction in
expenditure on economic and social activities."[17]

Mr. T. J. Natarajan said that "the Indian delegation was
opposed to any proposal which might ultimately have the
effect of curtailing approved economic and social programs
in the developing countries."[18] In 1960, Mr. J. N. Sahni
feared that the increasing expenditure of the United Nations
might affect the developmental programs of the underdeveloped countries. He pointed out that "the underdeveloped countries had their own problems to solve; and if they
had to make further sacrifices in order to meet their international obligations, that might prevent them from fulfilling
their domestic obligations."[19] He thought that the burden on
the developing countries could be lessened by making the
economically advanced countries meet a larger portion of
the United Nations expenditure. He was of the view that
"under present conditions and in the period of prosperity
through which some of the richest countries were passing, it
should be possible to increase some voluntary contributions

[17] United Nations, General Assembly, Sixth Session, *Official Records*,
Fifth Committee, 287th meeting, item 41 (16 November 1951) (Paris,
1952), p. 16. In 1957, Mr. Venkataraman thought that a reduction in the
United Nations' budget would affect the Organization's economic pro-
grams and the economic progress of developing states. See United
Nations, General Assembly, Eleventh Session, *Official Records*, Fifth
Committee, 543rd meeting, agenda item 65 (5 December 1956) (New
York, 1957), p. 61. See also I.C.W.A. Study, *op. cit.*, pp. 202-203. Mr.
Husain maintained that the United Nations' economic and social activi-
ties were necessary because the organization had to retain "its dynamic
character." See United Nations, General Assembly, Seventeenth Session,
Official Records, Fifth Committee, 923rd meeting, agenda item 62 (11
October 1962) (New York, 1963), p. 50.

[18] United Nations, General Assembly, Eleventh Session, *Official Records*, Fifth Committee, 595th meeting, agenda item 43 (22 February
1957) (New York, 1957), p. 46.

[19] United Nations, General Assembly, Fifteenth Session, Part I, *Official Records*, Fifth Committee, 776th meeting, agenda item 50 (27 October 1960) (New York, 1961), p. 86.

considerably and to assess the burden according to capacity to pay."[20] Mr. Menon came forth with the suggestion that the United Nations should levy the more advanced countries like the United States and the Soviet Union. He wanted the funds so collected to be administered by a special body of the United Nations to promote the economic development of the underdeveloped countries.[21] India maintained that economic development through the United Nations was as important as the maintenance of peace and security. In 1963, Mr. B. N. Chakravarty referred to the expenditure that the United Nations was incurring on peace-keeping operations and stated that "economic advancement must not be neglected merely because the Organization was facing a financial crisis resulting from heavy expenditure on such operations."[22]

FINANCING PEACE-KEEPING OPERATIONS

In India's view the expenses incurred by the United Nations on peace-keeping operations should be borne by the Organization as a whole. Mr. Venkataraman referred to the Secretary-General's statement which considered the financing of the United Nations Emergency Force (UNEF) and pointed out that "the Secretary-General made it abundantly

[20] *Ibid.*

[21] United Nations, General Assembly, Fifteenth Session, Part I, *Official Records,* 906th plenary meeting, agenda item 9 (17 October 1960) (New York, 1961), p. 749. In 1955, Mr. Menon favored the establishment of a special fund to promote economic development. See "Assembly's Great Debate Keyed to Geneva Spirit," *United Nations Review,* Vol. 2, No. 5 (November 1955), p. 62. Mr. B. Shiva Rao held that out of Indian proposals at the United Nations there emerged a positive scheme for the creation of the Special Fund. See *The Times,* London, January 21, 1961, p. iii.

[22] United Nations, General Assembly, Eighteenth Session, *Official Records,* Fifth Committee, 1029th meeting, agenda item 58 (31 October 1963) (New York, 1964), p. 113.

clear that the expenses of the Emergency Force other than for such pay, equipment, supplies and services as might be furnished without charge by member-states would have to be borne by the United Nations."[23] While maintaining in principle that peace-keeping expenses should be shared by all the member-states, India insisted that the developed countries should shoulder a large share of the expenses. Mr. Venkataraman stated that "the Indian delegation felt that the expenditures required for the maintenance of peace and security were imposing an increasing burden on the smaller and less developed countries, preventing them from participating further in the economic and social programs of the United Nations. The more advanced countries, which made large contributions to those programs, might make larger voluntary contributions in respect of measures to maintain peace and security in order to reduce the financial burdens of the less fortunate countries."[24] Mr. Menon also mentioned the burdens upon countries like India in maintaining peace-keeping forces. He wanted the question to be considered whether it would be possible for great countries, who have the capacity to make large contributions, to lessen the financial burden on poor countries like India.[25]

The Indian delegation felt that the costs of the Congo operations was high and stated that "the burden will fall heavily on many members who are economically and financially not so fortunate as others. It is desirable that the burden on the less wealthy nations should be lightened as far as possible.

[23] United Nations, General Assembly, Eleventh Session, *Official Records,* Fifth Committee, 555th meeting, agenda item 66 (18 December 1956) (New York, 1957), p. 131. See also United Nations, General Assembly, Fourteenth Session, *Official Records, Annexes,* agenda item 28 (Documents A/4176 and Add. 1 and 2), (New York, 1960), p. 17.

[24] United Nations, General Assembly, Thirteenth Session, *Official Records,* Fifth Committee, 664th meeting, agenda item 44 (21 October 1958) (New York, 1959), p. 78.

[25] United Nations, General Assembly, Thirteenth Session, *Official Records,* 774th plenary meeting, agenda item 9 (7 October 1958) (New York, 1959), p. 366.

We consider that for the Congo operations there should be a special scale of contributions, different from the assessments in regard to the regular expenses under Article 17 of the Charter."[26] Mr. B. N. Chakravarty insisted that it was particularly important that the factor of the reduced capacity to pay of the less developed countries should be taken into consideration in assessing contributions and warned that it would be dangerous to ignore it.[27]

India favored a special scale of assessments on peace-keeping expenses for alleviating the burden on the less developed countries. The Indian delegation stated in 1961 that "expenses of peace-keeping operations, particularly when viewed against the increasing cost of the United Nations membership being likely to prove an unconscionable burden on non-affluent states, should be apportioned in a manner which would cause the least burden and 'dis-incentive' to their membership and active participation in the United Nations."[28] India desired that assessments on peace-keeping op-

[26] United Nations, General Assembly, Fifteenth Session, *Official Records, Annexes,* Vol. 11, agenda items 49/50 (Document A/C.5/863, 14 April 1961) (New York, 1961), p. 34. See also United Nations, General Assembly, Sixteenth Session, *Official Records,* Fifth Committee, 905th meeting, agenda item 55 (15 December 1961) (New York, 1962), p. 329.

[27] United Nations, General Assembly, Fourth Special Session, *Official Records,* Fifth Committee, 994th meeting, agenda item 7 (6 June 1963) (New York, 1963), p. 60.

[28] United Nations, General Assembly, Sixteenth Session, *Official Records, Annexes,* Vol. 111, agenda item 62 (Document A/4971, 15 November 1961) (New York, 1962), p. 9. See also Swadesh Mehta, p. 225. Mr. S. K. Singh explained in 1963 that India favored a special scale of assessments with regard to peace-keeping expenses because India believed that such a method would reduce the contributions of the developing countries. See United Nations, General Assembly, Eighteenth Session, *Official Records,* Fifth Committee, 1057th meeting, agenda item 19 (13 December 1963) (New York, 1964), p. 288. India desired the application of a special assessment scale to all United Nations expenses which were not provided for in the regular budget. *Ibid.* Mr. Venkataraman contended that without a special scale of assessments on the peace-keeping expenses, the developing countries would be unable to fulfill their obligations. See United Nations, General Assembly, Sixteenth Session, *Official Records,* Fifth Committee, 858th meeting, agenda item 54 (18 December 1961) (New York, 1962), p. 59.

erations should reflect the capacity of member states to pay. The Indian and six other delegations of less developed states stated that "the special scale should be based on the principle of increasing the share of certain Member States and decreasing the share of certain other Member States according to the magnitude of the amount of the expenditures concerned."[29] India contended that the larger the volume of peace-keeping expenses, the larger should be the share of the permanent members of the Security Council and the economically developed members of the United Nations because their capacity to pay was greater.[30]

Although India considered that the peace-keeping expenses were the expenses of the United Nations as a whole and desired the developed countries to bear a large proportion of the expenditure, she held the view that the General Assembly could not require states to assume binding obligations. For instance, the Indian delegation contended that the United Nations operations in the Congo were not undertaken in accordance with Article 43 of the Charter and so there was no binding obligation on member states to finance the ONUC. Mr. Venkataraman explained that "while the activities of the United Nations in the Congo undoubtedly came within the scope of Chapter VII of the Charter, certain provisions of that Charter had not been complied with. Article 43, for example, provided for special agreements between the Security Council and United Nations members when the Council took certain measures for the maintenance of international peace and security. The fact that no special agreements had been concluded strengthened the argument

[29] United Nations, General Assembly, Fourth Special Session, *Official Records, Annexes,* agenda item 7 (Document A/Ac.113/18, 15 March 1963) (New York, 1963), p. 34.

[30] *Ibid.* See also United Nations, General Assembly, Sixteenth Session, *Official Records, Annexes,* Vol. 111, agenda item 62 (Document A/4971, 15 November 1961) (New York, 1962), p. 9.

that the Charter could not be cited as authority for imposing the financial responsibility for ONUC on the member states."[31] In India's view the expenses over peace-keeping operations were different from the regular expenses of the United Nations and as such they should be kept separate. Referring to the UN expenditures in the Congo, Mr. C. S. Jha stated that "the Congo operations are obviously of an extraordinary nature. They have a special purpose which is different from that of the normal regular expenses of the Organization. We do not think as a matter of principle, that it would be logical and right to bring within the framework of Article 17 of the Charter, the expenses in relation to a special and extraordinary undertaking like the Congo operations. . . . It seems to us reasonable to hold that Article 17 does not apply to such operations which must, therefore, be paid for by special arrangements decided in each case by the General Assembly, whose members must take their decisions bearing in mind their collective responsibility for peace and security."[32] While accepting the principle of collective responsibility in financing peace-keeping operations, Indian spokesmen refused to make it mandatory for member-states to pay their contributions.

India's doubts about the binding nature of the assessments over peace-keeping operations did not inhibit her representatives from emphasizing the responsibility of member states in meeting their financial obligations. Preferring not to define the nature of the United Nations expenditure on ONUC, Mr. C. S. Jha urged the General Assembly, in April 1961, to do something immediately "which will enable the prolonga-

[31] United Nations, General Assembly, Fifteenth Session, Part I, *Official Records,* Fifth Committee, 817th meeting, agenda item 49 (13 December 1960) (New York, 1961), p. 321. Mr. Jha opposed the idea of forcing a great power to pay for the United Nations peace-keeping operations. *Ibid.*

[32] General Assembly (Document A/C S/863, 14 April 1961), p. 34.

tion and the continuation of the operations, whatever might be the views of members of the Organization concerning their share of costs; it is in the interest of the entire organization to continue it and to have it concluded successfully."[33] Mr. Jha pointed out that states had a responsibility to share the expenses of the ONUC even if they had reservations about its functioning. He stated that the United Nations had about 20,000 troops and a large staff in the Congo and held that they had to be fed and provisioned. Appealing to the delegations to finance the Congo operations he stressed that the United Nations "has undertaken a tremendous responsibility. Some may think that that responsibility may have been wrongly taken, nevertheless it has the sanction of the Assembly and of the Security Council. We made the decisions and we must go through with it."[34]

In 1962 Mr. Husain thought the financing of the United Nations peace-keeping operations "raised a highly complex political problem which could be resolved only by lengthy negotiations within the General Assembly."[35] Indian spokesmen felt that an understanding among the great powers about the financing of peace-keeping operations was necessary to solve the United Nations financial problems. In 1965,

[33] United Nations, General Assembly, Fifteenth Session, Part 11, *Official Records,* 995th plenary meeting, agenda item 50 (21 April 1961) (New York, 1962), p. 85. India maintained that the Congo operations were essential for the maintenance of peace and security and for assisting the Congo and wanted the operations to continue until the fulfillment of the mission entrusted to the United Nations. See (Document A/C.5/863, 14 April 1961), p. 34. In 1962, Mr. Husain expressed a similar view and said that "it was of the utmost importance that all member states should pay their contributions to all United Nations accounts so as to enable the Organization to carry out its functions." See United Nations, General Assembly, Seventeenth Session, *Official Records,* Fifth Committee, 923rd meeting, agenda item 62 (11 October 1962) (New York, 1963), p. 49.

[34] *Ibid.*

[35] United Nations, General Assembly, Seventeenth Session, *Official Records,* Fifth Committee, 923rd meeting, agenda item 62 (11 October 1962) (New York, 1963), p. 49. In 1963, Mr. Chakravarty expressed the same view. See "Budget Estimates for 1964," *United Nations Review,* Vol. 11, No. 1 (January 1964), p. 44.

Prime Minister Shastri urged the United States and the Soviet Union to "evolve a formula to settle the issue of assessments."[36] India contended that with regard to solving the problem of arrears in contributions, there was no practical alternative to voluntary contributions.[37] The Indian delegation expressed appreciation of those developed countries that made voluntary contributions toward the United Nations peace-keeping expenses in the Congo and hoped that the flow of such contributions would not only be maintained but would be increased.[38]

India recognized that peace-keeping operations were essential and considered that all states should financially support such operations. Mr. B. N. Chakravarty argued that "if the United Nations was to fulfill its primary task of maintaining international peace and security, peace-keeping operations were, in certain circumstances, essential and obligatory. As operations of the United Nations, they must be paid for by the United Nations and since any United Nations action could only result from collective discussion, the expenditure must be the collective responsibility of all Members of the United Nations, irrespective of and without prejudice to the views held by various members."[39] Urging states to contribute finances to the United Nations peace-keeping activities, he stated that "the errors of the past must be forgotten and an attempt be made to make the organization more effective as a peace-keeping instrument."[40] In 1963, Mr. Chakravarty appealed "to all member states, irrespective

[36] *The New York Times,* February 15, 1965, p. 2.

[37] General Assembly (Document A/AC.121/SR.4, 27 April 1965), p. 44. See also *India News,* July 23, 1965, p. 1.

[38] General Assembly (Document A/C.5/863, 14 April 1961), p. 35.

[39] United Nations, General Assembly, Sixteenth Session, *Official Records, Annexes,* Vol. 111, agenda item 62 (Document A/4971, 15 November 1961) (New York, 1962), p. 9.

[40] United Nations, General Assembly, Fourth Special Session, *Official Records,* Fifth Committee, 994th meeting, agenda item 7 (6 June 1963) (New York, 1963), p. 59.

of their legal position or their views concerning the manner in which the peace-keeping operations had been conducted thus far, to come immediately to the help of the United Nations in its present serious difficulty."[41] He pointed out that India, by contributing fully to the expenses of the UNEF and the ONUC despite her reservations,[42] had "demonstrated the importance it attached to the financial stability of the United Nations and its effectiveness as a peace-keeping instrument."[43] He said that Guinea, after expressing dissatisfaction with the functioning of the ONUC, had agreed to pay up its arrears for the good of the Organization. He thought that the attitude adopted by the Guinean delegation was worthy of emulation.

India held the view that the peace-keeping expenses, in the absence of special agreements provided for under Article 43 of the Charter, should be apportioned by the General Assembly and not by the Security Council. India maintained that "the appropriations as well as the apportionment of expenditure for peace-keeping operations imposing financial liability on all members of the United Nations must be decided upon by the General Assembly itself like all other expenditures of the United Nations."[44] Pointing to those delegations which insisted that the peace-keeping expenses should be apportioned by the Security Council, Mr. S. K. Singh of the Indian delegation argued that "it would indeed be difficult for the 100 countries which were not members of the Security Council to accept an assessment in which they

[41] *Ibid.*

[42] "Easing the Financial Situation," *United Nations Review,* Vol. 10, No. 7 (July, 1963), pp. 13-14.

[43] United Nations, General Assembly, Seventeenth Session, *Official Records,* Fifth Committee, 972nd meeting, agenda item 62 (12 December 1962) (New York, 1963), p. 342.

[44] United Nations, General Assembly, Sixteenth Session, *Official Records, Annexes,* Vol. 111, agenda item 62 (Document A/4971, 15 November 1961) (New York, 1962), p. 9.

would have had no say. Should the members of the Security Council agree to share the financial burden among themselves, the other member states would no doubt be very happy, but it must be acknowledged that as the costs had to be shared among all the members of the Organization, it was for all member states to decide how they should be apportioned."[45] In India's view the financing of future peace-keeping operations should be based either on voluntary contribution or on compulsory assessments. India expressed opposition to a proposal to give the permanent members of the Security Council the option of not paying for those peace-keeping operations of which they did not approve.[46]

India's policy toward financing the United Nations was characterized by her insistence on a reduction of her contribution and a demand for increasing the contributions of the developed countries. India advocated an assessment system based on progressive taxation principles. While India wanted to make the rich nations pay a large proportion of the United Nations expenses, she also attempted to derive economic advantages by advocating the extension of United Nations economic assistance programs. Although India did not favor heavy increases in the United Nations budget, she considered that the peace-keeping and other activities of the United Nations were essential and should be carried out. While resisting proposals to make contributions toward peace-keeping operations legally obligatory, she maintained

[45] United Nations, General Assembly, Eighteenth Session, *Official Records*, Fifth Committee, 1057th meeting, agenda item 19 (13 December 1963) (New York, 1964), p. 288. Mr. Chakravarty reiterated this position in 1965 and added that "once the Security Council took a decision on any peace-keeping operation and failed to make any financial arrangements under Article 43 or otherwise, it should be the responsibility of the General Assembly to find the means for financing that operation and to apportion the costs involved among members." See General Assembly (Document A/AC. 121/SR.4, 27 April 1965), p. 44.

[46] *The New York Times*, April 28, 1965, p. 2.

that the expenses were the expenses of the United Nations and all members had a responsibility in financing such operations. In the event of differences over the financing of peace-keeping operations, Indian delegates maintained that the minority after expressing its objections over a peace-keeping operation should agree to pay its assessment toward such an operation in the interests of the UN and world peace.

6

India and
the United Nations Secretariat

India has taken a keen interest in the administrative aspect
of the United Nations. Her policy toward the Secretariat has
been characterized by her demand for greater representation
of Indians and Afro-Asians in the administration. She advocated a strong and independent secretariat and favored the
retention of the office of the Secretary-General under a single
individual.

THE DEMAND FOR MORE POSITIONS IN THE SECRETARIAT

The urge for active participation in the United Nations
led India to bid for the inclusion of a greater number of
Indians in the Secretariat. It was considered in India that

the Secretariat was a vital part of the United Nations and vast opportunities existed for the useful exercise of its functions. Indians contended that the inadequate representation for Asians in the Secretariat was a great handicap to India for "deriving the full benefit from the UNO."[1] The belief in the inadequacy of representation for India in the Secretariat prompted Mr. S. K. Kripalani of the Indian delegation to point out in 1946 that "India was not fairly represented on the staff. His country, whose population equalled approximately one-fifth of the human race, could offer persons of the highest calibre with the finest educational background as candidates for some of the senior posts in the Secretariat."[2] Mr. Krishna Menon reiterated this position in 1954 and said that the geographical distribution of posts in the higher echelons of the Secretariat was unsatisfactory. He stressed that "the Asian countries, which had old civilizations and vast populations, should be equitably represented in the ranks of the Secretariat up to the highest level."[3] The emphasis was shifted from the demand for equitable distribution of the posts in the Secretariat to the demand for position in the higher echelons of the administration. Mr. Menon contended that the whole of Asia "was represented by no more than six officers in the Principal Officers and Director cate-

[1] "U.N.O. Secretariat," *The Eastern Economist,* December 20, 1946, p. 997. Jam Sahib of Nawanagar expressed a similar view in 1948. See United Nations, General Assembly, Third Session, Part I. *Official Records,* Fifth Committee, 106th meeting (27 September 1948) (Paris, 1949), p. 16.

[2] United Nations, General Assembly, First Session, Second Part, *Official Records,* Fifth Committee, 41st meeting (11 December 1946) (Lake Success, 1948), p. 241.

[3] United Nations, General Assembly, Ninth Session, *Official Records,* Fifth Committee, 439th meeting, agenda items 53 and 38 (15 October 1954) (New York, 1955), p. 54. Mr. Nehru held the same view. He said that more Asians should have Secretariat posts, particularly in the principal officer category. See *The New York Times,* August 17, 1955, p. 15.

gories and only half of the quota allotted to Asian countries was filled by nationals of those countries."[4]

Indian delegates believed that the West was overrepresented in the Secretariat causing an imbalance in the Secretariat in favor of the West. India considered that the international character of the Secretariat could be maintained by minimizing the Western domination in the Secretariat and by distributing the positions on a geographical basis. In 1957, Mr. J. N. Sahni held that the imbalance had not yet been rectified, particularly at the top policy making level, and "considered it important that the United Nations Secretariat should become truly international."[5] In accordance with this objective India attempted to reduce the imbalance. Mr. Menon thought that "one way of removing the disparity in geographical representation would be to pay more attention to staffing regional offices on a nationality basis. Again, officials holding top level posts should be retired early."[6] Mr. P. P. Pillai regarded the geographical distribution of the staff as disturbing and suggested that "until balance had been restored, to confine recruitment mainly to unrepresented or under-represented countries."[7] In 1961, Mr. Ven-

[4] United Nations, General Assembly, Ninth Session, *Official Records,* Fifth Committee, 459th meeting, agenda item 53 (12 November 1954) (New York, 1955), p. 181.

[5] United Nations, General Assembly, Twelfth Session, *Official Records,* Fifth Committee, 629th meeting, agenda item 51 (27 November 1957) (New York, 1958), p. 152.

[6] United Nations, General Assembly, Tenth Session, *Official Records,* Fifth Committee, 522nd meeting, agenda item 38 (5 December 1955) (New York, 1956), p. 199.

[7] United Nations, General Assembly, Second Session, *Official Records,* Fifth Committee, 91st meeting (7 November 1947) (Lake Success, 1948), p. 364. He contended that India and Pakistan were entitled to seventy-five posts in the Secretariat, but the number of their nationals in the Secretariat amounted to ten. *Ibid.,* p. 365. Mr. R. Venkataraman complained in 1957 that due regard was not given to the under-represented countries in the promotion policy and requested the Secretary-

kartaraman pointed out the preponderance of the staff from North America and Western Europe and said that the situation was not in keeping with the adequate representations of the cultures, traditions, and customs of the various regions as envisaged in the Charter. He was in favor of providing definite guidance to the Secretary-General for accomplishing equitable geographical distribution of posts in the Secretariat "so that the smaller countries could play a larger part in the administration of the Organization."[8]

Since India regarded the Secretariat as an important organ of the United Nations, she considered that there should be an impact of every part of the world on it. While demanding a proper representation of the underrepresented states, Mr. Menon explained that "there should be a healthy and equitable impact of the various parts of the world."[9] The Indian delegation considered the principle of geographical distribution of positions in the Secretariat as a basic principle and held that the United Nations recruitment policy should be based on it. Mr. Venkataraman observed that "the principle of equitable geographical distribution in the recruitment of

General to achieve a better geographical distribution of posts. See United Nations, General Assembly, Eleventh Session, *Official Records,* Fifth Committee, 563rd meeting, agenda item 43 (8 January 1957) (New York, 1957), p. 178.

[8] United Nations, General Assembly, Sixteenth Session, *Official Records,* Fifth Committee, 889th meeting, agenda item 64 (24 November 1961) (New York, 1962), p. 247. Two years earlier, he requested the Secretary-General "to ensure the equitable geographical distribution of the staff." See United Nations, General Assembly, Fourteenth Session, *Official Records,* Fifth Committee, 740th meeting, agenda item 54 (9 November 1959) (New York, 1960), p. 167. Mr. Sahni thought it was the Secretary-General's duty to ensure that the Secretariat reflected the composition of the Organization. See United Nations, General Assembly, Fifteenth Session, Part I, Fifth Committee, 176th meeting, agenda item 50 (27 October 1960) (New York, 1961), p. 86.

[9] United Nations, General Assembly, Tenth Session, *Official Records,* 533rd plenary meeting, agenda item 9 (4 October 1955) (New York, 1956), p. 235.

staff had been included in the Charter as an obligation and not merely as a guide to recruitment."[10] He thought that "the ever-increasing obligation of the United Nations in different parts of the world could not be adequately fulfilled unless the various regions with distinctive political and social characteristics were represented in the staff."[11] India not only called for greater representation for the Afro-Asians in the Secretariat but also claimed that the nationals of the less developed countries were better suited for service with the United Nations. Mr. Menon questioned the argument that a country's contribution to the regular budget of the United Nations should determine the distribution of Secretariat posts. He challenged the contention that a country could not offer human material of great worth because it was economically poor. He said that the Secretariat should tap talent wherever it might be found. He hoped that in considering any of the top level appointments "the Secretary-General would bear in mind the fact that great international responsibilities were often best laid upon the shoulders of nationals of less powerful and smaller countries, less liable to be affected by considerations of political power."[12] In 1963, Mr. S. K. Singh recognized that considerable progress had been made with regard to the geographical distribution of Secretariat posts. At the same time he regarded the demand for specific posts by each delegation and the placing of emphasis on national interests as an unfortunate development. He said that the Secretary-General should be given a measure of latitude and discretion in implementing the broad objective

[10] United Nations, General Assembly, Fifteenth Session, Part I, *Official Records,* Fifth Committee, 792nd meeting, agenda item 60 (16 November 1960) (New York, 1961), p. 181.

[11] *Ibid.*

[12] United Nations, General Assembly, Ninth Session, *Official Records,* Fifth Committee, 459th meeting, agenda item 53 (12 November 1954) (New York, 1955), p. 181.

of geographical distribution of positions in the Secretariat.[13] While objecting to placing emphasis on national interests in personnel matters, India seemed to have attempted to further her own interests. Besides India's desire to let the Secretary-General exercise discretion over recruitment, she was promoting her own interests in deprecating the emphasis on national interests. India could hardly obtain any more positions if the Secretariat posts were to be distributed on a national basis. India's policy makers probably perceived that India could gain a greater number of positions if recruitment was to be made on the basis of merit from each geographical division. India's persistent demand for increased representation showed that India was eager to place her nationals in the Secretariat. India's recurrent requests for a share in the United Nations administration stemmed from her desire for recognition in world affairs and her desire for participation in the United Nations.

THE ADVOCACY OF AN INDEPENDENT SECRETARIAT

India desired that the Secretariat should be free from political pressures. She insisted on providing an efficient administrative machinery for the United Nations. At the Third Session the delegation of India favored a central recruitment agency for the whole United Nations and held that appointments should be made on the basis of merit. It wanted the United Nations, while recruiting personnel, to consider, the candidates' knowledge of the various parts of

[13] United Nations, General Assembly, Eighteenth Session, *Official Records,* Fifth Committee, 1049th meeting, agenda item 66 (29 November 1963) (New York, 1964), p. 241. While the Indian delegation desired to obtain more positions for Indians in 1946, the emphasis was shifted to a demand for the distribution of seats on the basis of geography in 1963.

the world where United Nations policies were being carried out, the candidates' character, their intellectual ability and impartiality.[14] In 1953, Mr. Rajeswar Dayal of the Indian delegation contended that "the provisions of the Charter leave us with no alternative but that of a truly international Secretariat in which competence, efficiency, integrity and equitable geographical distribution are the only principles which can be properly applied."[15]

India considered that the rights of the United Nations' personnel should be guaranteed and protected. She emphasized the importance of maintaining the morale of the staff and cautioned against discussing the question of dismissal of the administrative personnel. Mr. Adarkar viewed that "permanent officials should to all intents and purposes be irremovable, whereas it should be possible to dismiss temporary officials when the Secretary-General regarded it as essential."[16] India offered support for the independence of the Secretariat by vehemently opposing the concept of "host country." Mr. Rajeswar Dayal bitterly criticized the "host country" principle. He did not consider it to be a suitable method in United Nations' personnel policy. Mr. Dayal argued that the "host country" principle accorded "a special kind of treatment to the nationals of one particular coun-

[14] United Nations, General Assembly, Third Session, Part I, *Official Records*, Fifth Committee, 106th meeting (27 September 1948) (Paris, 1949), p. 16. Indian delegation maintained that the United Nations should follow the normal personnel principles in its recruitment policy. The Jam Sahib of Nawanagar insisted on the advertisement of the posts to be filled and qualifications required, the interview of qualified candidates and the acceptance of the recommendation of the Bureau of Personnel or the Board concerned. *Ibid.*

[15] United Nations, General Assembly, Seventh Session, *Official Records*, 416th plenary meeting, agenda item 75 (28 March 1953) (New York, 1953), p. 565.

[16] United Nations, General Assembly, Sixth Session, *Official Records*, Fifth Committee, 332nd meeting, item 45 (22 January 1952) (Paris, 1952), pp. 288-289.

try."[17] According to him the host country principle was not a valid one or one capable of constructive application to personnel policies in the Secretariat. In this regard he pointed out that "the members of the staff of the United Nations, no matter from what country they are drawn, owe their loyalty to the United Nations."[18] However, he explained at the same time, the members of the United Nations Secretariat should not indulge in subversive activities directed against any state. Like Mr. Dayal, Mr. Menon also maintained that "a civil servant, international or otherwise, must remain non-political, non-partisan and not concerned with action against any party who may be a client of the Organization as a whole."[19]

Opposing the Advisory Committee's suggestion that permanent contracts should be subject to scrutiny every five years, Mr. Ali Yawar Jung said that it "would undoubtedly create a deplorable state of uncertainty and anxiety in the Secretariat."[20] India maintained that the United Nations could not discharge its employees without showing a proper cause. Indian delegates stressed that employees had the right to request a review of disputes in which they were involved. Referring to the administration's authority with regard to the dismissal of employees, an Indian delegate argued that "the United Nations action must depend on the policy determined by the General Assembly; and in any event, what was essen-

[17] General Assembly, 416th plenary meeting (28 March 1953), *op. cit.*, p. 507. According to the "host country" principle, the United Nations' employees had a special responsibility to the country in which they were stationed.

[18] *Ibid.*

[19] United Nations, General Assembly, Seventh Session, *Official Records*, 422nd plenary meeting, agenda item 75 (1 April 1953) (New York, 1953), p. 665.

[20] United Nations, General Assembly, Eighth Session, *Official Records*, Fifth Committee, 414th meeting, item 51 (28 November 1953) (New York, 1954), p. 241. He expressed satisfaction with the policy pursued by Secretary-General Hammarskjold in safeguarding the rights of the Secretariat personnel.

tially a matter for proper investigation by United Nations authorities."[21] Indian delegates favored an employee being provided every access to present his case and to attain fair judicial redress.

India held the view that the final authority to settle a dispute between the Secretary-General and an employee of the United Nations rested with the Administrative Tribunal. An Indian delegate contended in 1953 that "the Statute of the Tribunal, as it stood, conferred on the Administrative Tribunal the competence it had exercised in reversing the Secretary-General's decisions in the cases in question, and also competence to assess and order the payment of compensation. The Tribunal was the judge of its own competence, and according to its statute, its decisions were final. The legal question whether in the final resort the General Assembly had the right to review, revise or reverse the Tribunal's decisions did not arise, for even if, in theory, it might be said to exist, it would not and should not be exercised in practice except for the gravest reasons."[22] He firmly believed in the superiority of the Administrative Tribunal over the executive authority in matters pertaining to personnel disputes and strongly defended the powers of the Tribunal. Addressing the Fifth Committee, he stated that "it should always be borne in mind that the creation of the Administrative Tri-

[21] United Nations, General Assembly, Eighth Session, *Official Records, Fifth Committee*, 425th meeting, item 38 (7 December 1953) (New York, 1954), p. 323.

[22] *Ibid.* In his view the General Assembly was not suited to act as a judicial body. He held that "the General Assembly was not the proper forum to deal with questions of law, much less to examine individual cases from that viewpoint." *Ibid.*, p. 324. The same view was expressed at the Ninth Session. Mr. Sapru said that the General Assembly "cannot, in the very nature of things, act as a judicial body; discussions there are likely subsequently to prejudice seriously a fair trial of the issues between the staff member and the Organization." See United Nations, General Assembly, Ninth Session, *Official Records*, 515th plenary meeting, agenda item 53, 48, 73 and 38 (17 December 1954) (New York, 1955), p. 544.

bunal had given the United Nations staff an important
guarantee of the contracted relations between the Organization and its employees, particularly as regards the implementation of the staff regulations."[23]

Indian delegates expressed concern at the attempts to
interfere in the independence and integrity of the Secretariat.
They were favorably inclined toward the development of an
international civil service through the United Nations. Mr.
Krishna Menon stated that "it would not be right for any
country, however great or however small, to interfere in the
integrity or in the development of an international civil
service, which is probably one of the great contributions we
can make towards world citizenship. So when the appropriate
time comes, we shall look forward to the Secretary-General
upholding the integrity of the Secretariat, permitting no
inroads upon it and allowing no construction of legalisms,
except after thorough examination, to invade the individual's
responsibility or the loyalty of the Secretariat to this international Organization."[24]

During the Ninth Session Mr. Sapru expressed the view
that the impartiality of an international civil service was an
asset of the highest value to the Organization. He desired
that an international civil servant must be objective. Mr.
Sapru thought that it would be unwise to recruit persons who
had played a prominent part in inter-state controversies or in
international disputes. He explained that "the international

[23] *Ibid.*, p. 324. Reiterating these views, he contended in 1954 that the
awards of the Administrative Tribunal were final and without appeal.
He warned that any review of a decision of the Tribunal could not fail
to have an undesirable effect on the morale of the staff and the efficiency
of the Secretariat. See United Nations, General Assembly, Ninth Session,
Official Records, Fifth Committee, 476th meeting, agenda item 48 (6
December 1954) (New York, 1955), p. 281.

[24] United Nations, General Assembly, Eighth Session, *Official Records,*
448th plenary meeting, agenda item 9 (28 September 1953) (New York,
1954), p. 203.

civil servant must not only be impartial and free from any bias but must also enjoy that reputation. He therefore urged that the healthy custom should be developed of reserving such positions not for politicians, statesmen, or diplomats who had taken part in international disputes, but for civil servants or experts who worked in a quiet, often unostentatious, but efficient manner, and brought to bear upon their duties the essential virtue of freedom from controversy."[25]

Emphasizing the international character of the United Nations civil service, Indian delegates considered that an employee of the Secretariat was a servant of the United Nations as a whole and not a servant of any particular state. Mr. Sapru contended that parties to an appeal, on decisions relating to personnel disputes, could be the Secretary-General and the concerned staff member. He made it clear that India was "completely opposed to any discussion of a case on the initiative of any member or members before the General Assembly or the Fifth Committee."[26] He thought it to be contrary to the principles of jurisprudence and the principle of the international character of the United Nations "if a Member State were given the right of initiating or presenting reviews, revisions or appeals in cases in which staff members were concerned."[27] India's desire to keep the Secretariat free

[25] United Nations, General Assembly, Ninth Session, *Official Records,* Fifth Committee, 439th meeting, agenda items 53 and 38 (15 October 1954) (New York, 1955), p. 55. For the expression of the same view by Mr. Krishna Menon, see *Ibid.,* 459th meeting, agenda item 53 (12 November 1954), p. 181. While considering the question of objectivity on the part of the United Nations officials, Mr. Sapru insisted that the Secretariat personnel should not accept any part time work, and any honors and decorations even for services performed prior to their joining the Secretariat. See *Ibid.,* 469th meeting, agenda item 54 (26 November 1954), p. 243.

[26] General Assembly, 515th plenary meeting (17 December 1954) *op. cit.,* p. 544.

[27] *Ibid.,* p. 545. Mr. Menon referred to a recommendation of the Fifth Committee to allow states to initiate the review of cases on the verdicts of the Administrative Tribunal and to make the General Committee of the previous session as the screening committee over the appeals for the

from the interference of great powers and her fear that they would use the Secretariat for promoting their own interests led her to support the independence of the Secretariat. India's belief that the interests of the United Nations would be best served by a Secretariat not dominated or greatly influenced by powerful members of the Organization prompted her representatives to advocate the rights of the employees. National interest apart, idealism had an impact upon India's insistence on safeguarding the interests of the United Nations personnel and her favorable inclination toward promoting the concept of an international civil service.

ATTITUDE TOWARD THE
OFFICE OF THE SECRETARY-GENERAL

Indian spokesmen maintained that the office of the Secretary-General was a significant one and considered it as an important part of the United Nations system. Mr. Krishna Menon held the conviction that the Secretary-General had a crucial role to play in the maintenance of peace and security. He emphasized that "the office of the Secretary-General is a Charter organ of the United Nations. He has rights, he has obligations, he has functions, he has a status of his own."[28] At the time of the 1956 Hungarian crisis, Mr. Menon favored the Secretary-General paying a visit to Hungary to assess the situation. Claiming that the role of the Secretary-General was a broad one, he argued that if the Secretary-General wishes to visit any state he should be received by

review of cases, and considered it to be a "vicious" proposal because it would introduce a political element into a judicial procedure. See United Nations, General Assembly, Tenth Session, *Official Records,* 541st plenary meeting, agenda item 49 (8 November 1955) (New York, 1956), pp. 279-282.

[28] United Nations, General Assembly, Eleventh Session, *Official Records,* 586th plenary meeting, agenda item 67 (21 November 1956) (New York, 1957), p. 167.

that particular state. He felt that the Hungarian government should not obstruct the Secretary-General from exercising his responsibilities. Referring to the role that was bestowed on the Secretary-General by the Charter, Mr. Menon pointed out that "irrespective of his personality, great or small, he is endowed with all the functions which the Charter contemplates in one of its principal organs. We believe that every Member State has a moral duty . . . to accept the presence of the Secretary-General within its country at any time, unless there are reasons which affect the personal safety of the Secretary-General, in which case it should be open to him to take the risk or not to take it, just as he chooses."[29]

At the time of the Congo crisis, Indian leaders stood solidly in favor of retaining the Secretariat under a single individual. While expressing dissatisfaction with the way the United Nations peace-keeping operation in the Congo was conducted, India staunchly supported the institution of the Secretary-General. Referring to proposals for reorganizing the office of the Secretary-General, Mr. Nehru stated in 1960 that "insofar as executive action is concerned, it would not be desirable for the executive to be weakened when frequent and rapid decisions have to be made. That would mean an abdication of the responsibilities undertaken by the United Nations. If the executive itself is split up and pulls in different directions, it will not be able to function adequately or with speed. For that reason, the executive should be given authority to act within the terms of the directions issued."[30]

---

[29] *Ibid.*, 608th plenary meeting (4 December 1956) (New York, 1957), p. 522.

[30] Nehru, *India's Foreign Policy, op. cit.*, p. 223. At the same time he pointed out that the executive has to keep in view all the time the impact of various forces in the world." *Ibid.* Mr. Nehru desired the Secretary-General to consider various aspects before making a decision. *Ibid.*, p. 181. For a presentation of Mr. Nehru's views on the Soviet plan to replace the Secretary-General Dag Hammerskjold with a three man directorate, see *The New York Times,* October 4, 1960, p. 21. He reiterated this position in 1961 by saying that he "was opposed to having the Soviet

Mr. Krishna Menon was more emphatic on the question of the reorganization of the Secretariat on the basis of the Soviet proposals. He clearly stated that "we desire a United Nations that will function strongly. . . . we do not believe in an executive which provides for the functioning of three heads that would cancel out each other. Therefore, we are against a Secretariat which possesses these three heads."[31] Mr. Menon argued that the acceptance of the "Troika" would result in the violation of the Charter. He emphatically stated that "we do not support 'Troika' for the reason that we do not accept the division of the world into three parts and what is more, so far as the Secretary-General is concerned it goes contrary to the Charter."[32] India discouraged the Soviet Union from insisting on the reorganization of the Secretariat. Referring to India's position toward the "Troika" proposals, Palmer pointed out that India resisted Soviet attempts to weaken the United Nations, realizing, like other neutralist states, that there was "much to be gained in the present setup within the United Nations."[33]

The delegation of India played a significant role in the

Union raise now the issues of the replacement of Secretary-General Dag Hammarskjold and the reorganization of the Secretariat." See *The New York Times,* February 28, 1961, p. 1.

[31] United Nations, General Assembly, Sixteenth Session, *Official Records,* Vol. 1, 1025th plenary meeting, agenda item 9 (4 October 1961) (New York, 1962), p. 254. Mr. Menon felt that an individual occupying the office of the Secretary-General should be objective and must have the courage to express "correct" positions. *Ibid.,* p. 254. Expressing the same views, Mr. Nehru said that he "could not conceive of any joint functioning, any effective functioning, if there were three heads of this great institution." See *Rayjya Sabha Debates,* Vol. XXXI, 21 December 1960, column 2946, quoted in Rai, "Indian Attitude Toward the Revision of the United Nations Charter-11," *op. cit.,* p. 109. Mr. Nehru called the "Troika" proposal a "three headed god" and rejected it. See *The Times,* London, October 22, 1960, p. 4.

[32] *Lok Sabha Debates,* Second Series, Vol. LX, December 7, 1961, column 3938, quoted in Rai, "Indian Attitude Towards Revision of the United Nations Charter-11," *op. cit.,* pp. 109-110.

[33] Palmer, "The Afro-Asians in the United Nations," *op. cit.,* p. 128.

selection of a successor to Secretary-General Hammarskjold. It was reported that "India was pressing for a U.S.-Soviet agreement that the UN General Assembly should elect an interim Secretary-General who would have the same powers as the late Dag Hammarskjold."[34] When the question of the selection of a Secretary-General was successfully solved, Mr. Krishna Menon claimed that India made a significant contribution in resolving the deadlock over the appointment of the Secretary-General in 1961.[35] Congratulating Secretary-General U Thant, Mr. C. S. Jha said that he was confident that "the new Secretary-General would fill the office with dignity, ability, honor and impartiality."[36] He expressed gratification for retaining the institution of the Secretary-General as it was. He said that "we are very happy that the authority of the Secretary-General has been fully maintained. There has been no denigration of the position and of the authority that the Secretary-General has been given under the Charter."[37]

With regard to the appointment of the Secretary-General, Indian delegates maintained that the provisions of the Charter should be strictly observed. They emphasized that the recommendation of the Security Council was an essential requirement in appointing a Secretary-General. Opposing suggestions that the General Assembly, without the consent of the Security Council, appoint a Secretary-General, Mr. Menon argued that "we are not a member of the Security Council, but we are a member of this Organization and, therefore, if the Secretary-General is merely a creature of the

---

[34] *The New York Times*, September 28, 1961, p. 18.

[35] *Lok Sabha Debates*, Second Series, Vol. LX, 7 December 1961, col. 3939, quoted in Rai, "Indian Attitude Towards Revision of the United Nations Charter-11," *op. cit.*, p. 110.

[36] "U Thant of Burma Appointed Acting Secretary-General," *United Nations Review*, Vol. 8, No. 12 (December 1961), p. 18.

[37] *Ibid.*

General Assembly appointed by a majority vote in the Assembly or even a unanimous vote and not related to another Charter organ, the Security Council, it would put the Security Council outside the competence of the appointee and vice versa."[38]

India's reliance on the United Nations for implementing her foreign policy objectives and her satisfaction in realizing some of these objectives led Indian spokesmen to believe that they had a stake in the future of the Organization. India's realization in the usefulness of the United Nations roused her support for maintaining the Secretariat under a single Secretary-General. Indian policy makers and representatives desired the Secretariat to be strong, efficient and effective, and independent of great power pressures. While attempting to further India's own interests, Indian delegates sought to strengthen the Secretariat. During the 1960 Congo crisis India opposed the proposals to weaken the power of the Secretary-General. On the contrary India persistently urged the Secretary-General to pursue a more vigorous and assertive role in conducting the United Nations peace-keeping operation in the Congo. India's advocacy of the rights of the Secretariat employees and her efforts in safeguarding their privileges is an indication of India's support for the United Nations. India's insistence on retaining the institution of the Secretary-General and her demand for a vigorous role by the Secretary-General in the maintenance of peace and security shows India's interest in developing the United Nations into a strong and effective institution.

---

[38] General Assembly, 1025th plenary meeting (4 October 1961) *op. cit.,* p. 255. However, it must be pointed out here that when the Security Council failed to agree on an acceptable candidate to replace Mr. Trygvie Lie as Secretary-General in 1950, India supported a proposal to extend the term of Mr. Lie, by the General Assembly alone, for three years. See "Trygvie Lie Continued in Office," *United Nations Bulletin,* Vol. 9, No. 10 (November 15, 1950), p. 520.

7

Conclusion

India's policy at the United Nations toward amending the Charter, colonialism, the United Nations peace forces, financing and the Secretariat was aimed at promoting and maintaining India's influence in world affairs. The desire for recognition of her status was not an end in itself. India looked to the United Nations for implementing her foreign policy objectives.

India's policy toward issues at the United Nations was governed by her conception of the United Nations, as an international organization of sovereign states, working to realize the purposes of the Charter through the cooperative effort of its members. India desired the United Nations to become a broad-based Organization reflecting the realities of the world, and advocated the principle of universality of membership. India's belief in the existence of an imbalance in the United Nations and her desire to minimize the Western domination over the Organization led her to advocate the admission of all states into the United Nations. The efforts at reducing the imbalance stemmed from the belief that India's contribution, hence her influence, would be greater in an organization not dominated by any single bloc of powers.

The nationalist urge for recognition of India's position in the world inspired her policy-makers to follow a non-alignment approach to maximize her influence. Indian leaders chose neither neutrality nor isolation in foreign affairs but consciously sought a vigorous role for India at the United Nations.

While the desire for recognition of India's international status led her to participate actively in the United Nations, her active participation enabled her to utilize the Organization to implement her foreign policy objectives. India attempted to realize her policy goals through the United Nations. The pursuit of colonialism is a case in point. India found the United Nations a useful instrument to present India's policy on colonial issues. It was recognized by Indian leaders that the United Nations accelerated the process toward self-determination of dependent peoples. While demanding self-determination for those who were not yet independent, Indian spokesmen sought to win the good will of the educated sections in the colonial territories. The bodies of the United Nations served as useful forums in the pursuit of this objective. While India's objective to attain independence for subject peoples was beyond doubt, she was also attempting to maintain and promote her influence in the Afro-Asian world through her anti-colonial role at the United Nations.

It must be emphasized that India pursued a reciprocative anti-colonial role at the United Nations, simultaneously adopting postures of aggressiveness and moderation toward colonial issues. India exhibited extremism and, at the same time, showed a sense of sober responsibility throughout the history of the United Nations in response to the types of colonial policies pursued by metropolitan powers. India was intransigent toward a colonial policy which she considered to be repressive and was sympathetic toward a policy which she perceived to be liberal. India's consistent hostility toward Portuguese colonialism and sympathetic attitude toward British colonialism revealed the reciprocative element in India's anti-colonialism.

The desire for influence and the aspiration for participation in the United Nations were evident in India's attitude toward the amendment of the United Nations Charter. While looking with disdain upon Western efforts to amend the Charter, Indian delegates persistently, although cautiously, attempted to bring changes in the structure of the United Nations so as to secure greater representation for India and to the Afro-Asians in the councils and committees of the Organization. In 1963, along with other Afro-Asian countries, India succeeded in putting across a resolution in the General Assembly to expand the membership of the Security Council and the Economic and Social Council.

While desiring changes in the Charter, Indian diplomats insisted that understanding among the great powers was essential to revision of the Charter. India's resistance to the removal of the veto and opposition to making the General Assembly an enforcement agency, through the Uniting for Peace Resolution, stemmed from her conception of the United Nations. India considered that enforcement action was a prerogative of the Security Council and for such action unanimity among its permanent members was required. India's objections also stemmed from her belief in the existence of an imbalance in the Assembly and from her fear that the dominant bloc might employ the Assembly to further its own objectives to the disadvantage of others.

The request of the Secretary-General for India's participation in various peace-keeping activities provided opportunities to India to participate in the United Nations operations and, in the process, to enhance her influence. While contributing contingents to the UNEF and the ONUC, India significantly shaped the role and functions of the United Nations forces. India derived satisfaction from her participation in the various United Nations peace-keeping operations. Whenever these were brought more in line with India's views, her contribution of men and material to those operations was proportionately increased.

Indian policy makers and representatives were lukewarm toward proposals to establish a permanent United Nations force. Their belief in the existence of an imbalance in the General Assembly led them to oppose the creation of a permanent force. It was feared in India that the dominant group in the General Assembly might take advantage of the availability of a force and employ it against a great power. Indian spokesmen were also apprehensive that such a force might be used to the disadvantage of small states. Self-interest was the determining factor in Indian opposition to the formation of a permanent force. Apart from the insistence on the practical difficulties with regard to the formation of a permanent force, India's opposition stemmed from the belief of her representatives that she could have a greater voice over the functioning of an ad hoc force than over a permanent force. The desire to have a finger on the trigger in peace-keeping operations prompted Indian delegates to discourage proposals to set up a United Nations force on a permanent basis.

The Indian anxiety not to create any precedent that would likely threaten her position over Kashmir largely influenced India's policy toward the United Nations peace-keeping forces. Indians were suspicious of the fact that the United Nations, if a permanent force were to be available, might dispatch it to Kashmir. While contributing contingents to the UNEF and the ONUC, Indian leaders insisted on so many reservations, conditions and qualifications mainly to safeguard her position in Kashmir.

In her policy toward the financing of the United Nations system, Indian delegates maintained that the developed nations should bear a larger proportion of the expenses. They insisted that the assessment of contributions should be based on the principle of capacity to pay. In their view the greater the amount of expenditures, the larger should be the contribution of the economically advanced countries. While demanding a reduction in India's contribution, they constantly opposed reductions in the United States' contributions. The Indian delegation supported the economic undertakings of the United Nations. While showing concern at the constant increase in the United Nations expenditures, it advocated the approval of the budget estimates of the Secretariat for economic development. It was contended by Indian delegates that the economic programs of the organization were as important and essential as its peace-keeping activities.

While recognizing the expenses of peace-keeping operations as the expenses of the United Nations as a whole, the Indian delegation maintained that there was no binding legal obligation on members to pay for such expenses. However, the delegation of India felt that there was a responsibility on the part of members to make financial contributions to the Organization's peace-keeping operations. In India's view a state had every right to express reservations and misgivings over the functioning of an operation. After expressing its dissatisfaction about the functioning of a force, India held that a state should accept its financial responsibility and pay its contribution.

Desiring to reduce the burden on the less developed states, Indian delegates favored the establishment of a special scale of assessments, on the basis of a country's capacity to pay, to finance the peace-keeping operations. As for a solution to contributions in arrears, they thought that there was no alternative to voluntary contributions. It was suggested by India that the great powers should work out a formula to solve the Organization's financial crisis.

On the question of assessing expenditures for peace-keeping operations in the future, Indian delegates maintained that the General Assembly should be the apportioning body. They held that in the absence of special agreements, concluded by the Security Council in accordance with Article 43 of the Charter, the General Assembly should exercise the authority to apportion the expenses incurred for the peace-keeping operations.

The Indian demand for a greater number of Secretariat posts to Indians and Afro-Asians was a manifestation of India's desire for influence in world affairs and her aspiration for active participation in the United Nations. By insisting on equitable geographical distribution of positions in the Secretariat, Indian delegates were attempting to promote India's interests. In their policy toward the Secretariat, Indian delegates desired and attempted to reduce the domination of the Secretariat by individuals from the North American and West European continents.

While pointing to the lack of adequate representation of Afro-Asians in the Secretariat, particularly in the higher echelons of the administration, the Indian delegation assumed the role of an Afro-Asian spokesman. Indian representatives showed disinclination toward demands for a distribution of Secretariat posts on a national basis. They held the view that a region should be taken as a basis in the distribution of positions. A motivating factor in India's emphasis on regional allocation of Secretariat posts was the perception of Indian diplomats that she could obtain a greater number of positions in the United Nations Secretariat if the positions were to be filled on a regional basis.

There was an element of idealism in India's attitude toward the United Nations Secretariat. Indian delegates championed the rights and privileges of the Organization's employees. They strove to secure and safeguard the interests of the Secretariat personnel by advocating permanent tenure, increases in pay, and judicial protection. They also opposed political interference of member states in personnel matters. Perhaps idealism conditioned India's desire for developing an independent international Secretariat.

Indian leaders showed uninhibited support for the office of the Secretary-General. In India's view the Secretary-General had a significant role to play. During the 1956 Hungarian crisis, Mr. Krishna Menon argued that, upon request, the Secretary-General should be received by the Hungarian government. It was pointed out by Indian delegates that the Secretary-General was entitled under the Charter to perform certain responsibilities and it was wrong for any state to obstruct him from discharging his duties. In 1960 while expressing dissatisfaction with the way Secretary-General Hammarskjold was directing the United Nations operation in the Congo, India emphatically enunciated her intention to retain the office of the Secretary-General, under a single individual, as an effective and strong institution and vehemently opposed attempts to weaken the authority of the Secretary-General. On the contrary, Indian spokesmen urged Secretary-General Hammarskjold to follow a vigorous and effective policy in the Congo. They favored adherence to the provisions of the Charter in filling the office of the Secretary-General and maintained that the consent of the Security Council was essential in appointing a Secretary-General.

India's satisfaction with the usefulness of the United Nations and her belief that she had a stake in its future and development led her to support the organization. India opposed proposals like the "troika" because Indian leaders felt that such proposals would weaken the United Nations. India's support of the United Nations is understandable. With the major exception of Kashmir, the aims of Indian foreign policy and the objectives of the United Nations were in harmony. The United Nations furthered such Indian objectives as international peace, economic development of the developing states, securing of self-determination to dependent peoples and the projection of India's image in the world. The councils and committees of the United Nations provided countless opportunities that India so desperately needed to project her status in world affairs. The availability of opportunities for participation in the United Nations enabled India to play a vigorous role and to assert herself as the spokesman of the under-developed, the unaligned, and the hitherto voiceless continents of Asia and Africa. The satisfaction derived from the utilization of the United Nations logically led India to staunchly support the Organization.

Indian policy makers and representatives need the world body to present India's policies and to project her image in the international arena. The Indian instinct for an active role in world affairs seems to be gaining momentum under the leadership of Mrs. Indira Gandhi and Indians might very well utilize the United Nations to satisfy the urge for participation in world affairs. It is very likely that the United Nations will continue to promote the objectives that are espoused by India. Therefore, it is very likely that India will continue to support the United Nations.

It must be pointed out that there was a combination of both realism and idealism in India's foreign policy. Prime Minister Jawaharlal Nehru enunciated in 1954 that "a policy must be in keeping with the traditional background and

temper of the country. It should be idealistic, aiming at certain objectives, and, at the same time, it should be realistic.
If it is not idealistic, it becomes one of sheer opportunism;
if it is not realistic, then it is likely to be adventurist and
wholly ineffective."[1] There was more realism than idealism
in India's policy toward issues that came before the United
Nations. Referring to the Indian Government's instructions
to its representatives at the United Nations, Mr. Nehru
stated that "it is certainly true that our instructions to our
delegates have always been firstly, to consider each question
in terms of India's interest, secondly, on its merits—I mean
to say if it did not affect India."[2] In explaining India's policy
Nehru was neither paradoxical nor contradictory. To him
national interest was the primary factor determining policy.
On issues having to do with India's interests, he was "on his
country's side and nobody else's,"[3] including, perhaps, the
United Nations. Whether this attitude was an outgrowth of
nationalism or was based on political realism or enlightened
self-interest, in the final analysis it rested on securing advantages to one's own country. Mr. Nehru pointed out in the
Indian Parliament that "whatever policy you may lay down,
the art of conducting the foreign policy of a country lies in
finding out what is most advantageous to the country. We
may talk about international good will and mean what we
say. We may talk about peace and mean what we say. But in
the ultimate analysis a government functions for the ultimate
good of the country it governs and no government dare do

[1] *Congress Bulletin,* No. 5 (June-July 1954), p. 246. Quoted in Rajan,
op. cit., p. 212. Nehru added that India's approach was dictated by every
consideration of intelligent self-interest. According to Rajan India's policy
was determined by her "own enlightened national interest." *Ibid.*

[2] Nehru, *Independence and After, op. cit.,* p. 215. Mr. Nehru's qualifi-
cation obviously ruled out the consideration of a question "on its merits"
because every important issue that was considered at the United Nations
had a bearing, one way or another, on every member of the Organization.

[3] Nehru's *Jawaharlal Nehru Speeches 1949-53, op. cit.,* p. 187.

anything which in the short or long run is manifestly to the disadvantage of that country." Here Mr. Nehru almost sounded like a political opportunist, but in analyzing Indian foreign policy, he was not defining political opportunism. The fact of the matter was that Mr. Nehru, like any other head of a government, was conscious of his country's interests while formulating and conducting Indian foreign policy.

India's policy toward the issues under consideration could be meaningfully understood only in relation to India's perception of her national interest. The desire of Indian policymakers to gain advantages for India was manifested in India's policy at the United Nations. The advocacy of universality of membership, the demand for the reorganization of the councils of the Organization, the championing the cause of the colonial peoples, the reservations on peace-keeping forces, the emphasis on the Organization's economic programs and the insistence on the equitable geographical distribution of Secretariat posts were aimed to attain advantages to India.

Idealism also had its impact on India's policy. India's insistence on agreement among the great powers on Charter revision and enforcement action, her insistence on the total eradication of colonialism, her belief in the collective responsibility of member-states to finance the peace-keeping operations, and her support for an independent Secretariat and a strong institution of the office of Secretary-General, sprung from an idealism that was evident in India's foreign policy. While elements of realism and idealism were strikingly evident in India's policy toward all issues that have been considered, the former, however, played the determining role. The conception of India's national interest by Indian foreign-policy makers and diplomats and their desire to promote that interest largely determined India's policy at the United Nations.

Bibliography

UNITED NATIONS DOCUMENTS

General Assembly

Official Records of the General Assembly and its main Committees from the First Session (1946) to the Nineteenth Session (1965).

Security Council

United Nations. *Official Records of the Security Council, 941st Meeting.* New York, 1961.
United Nations. *Official Records of the Security Council, 952nd Meeting.* New York, 1961.

INDIAN PARLIAMENTARY DOCUMENTS

India. *Lok Sabha Debates* (3rd Series), Vol. III (1962).
India. *Lok Sabha Debates* (3rd Series), Vol. XXI (1963).
India. *Lok Sabha Debates* (3rd Series), Vol. XXXIV (1964).

Books

AZKIN, BENJAMIN. *New States and International Organizations.* Paris: UNESCO, 1955.

BERKES, ROSS N., AND BEDI, MOHINDER S. *The Diplomacy of India: Indian Foreign Policy in the United Nations.* Stanford: Stanford University Press, 1958.

BOWLES, CHESTER. *Ambassadors' Report.* New York: Harper and Bros., 1954.

BRECHER, MICHAEL. *Nehru: A Political Biography.* London: Oxford University Press, 1959.

EAYERS, JAMES G. *The Commonwealth and Suez, A Documentary Survey.* London: Oxford University Press, 1962.

Foreign Policy of India: Text of Documents, 1947–59. New Delhi: Loksabha Secretariat, 1959.

FRYE, WILLIAM R. *A United Nations Peace Force.* New York: Oceana Publications, 1957.

GEORGE, T. J. S. *Krishna Menon.* New York: Taplinger Publishing Company, 1964.

GUPTA, KARUNAKAR. *Indian Foreign Policy in Defense of National Interest.* Calcutta: The World Press, 1956.

KARUNAKARAN, K. P. *India in World Affairs, 1947–50.* London: Oxford University Press, 1952.

————. *India in World Affairs, 1950–53.* London: Oxford University Press, 1958.

————, (ed.). *Outside the Contest: A Study of Non-Alignment and the Foreign Policies of Some Non-Aligned Countries.* New Delhi: Peoples Publishing House, 1963.

KUNDRA, J. C. *Indian Foreign Policy 1947–1954.* Groningen, Netherlands: J. B. Wolters, 1955.

LEVI, WERNER. *Free India in Asia.* Minneapolis: University of Minnesota Press, 1952.

MITRA, N. N. (ed.). *Indian Annual Register,* II. Calcutta: N. N. Mitra, 1946.

MURTI, B. S. N. *Nehru's Foreign Policy*. New Delhi: The Beacon Information and Publications, 1953.

NEHRU, JAWAHARLAL. *Independence and After*. New Delhi: The Publications Division, Government of India, 1949.

————. *India's Foreign Policy*. New Delhi: The Publications Division, Government of India, 1961.

————. *Jawaharlal Nehru's Speeches: 1949–1953*. New Delhi: The Publications Division, Government of India, 1954.

————. *Jawaharlal Nehru's Speeches, IV*. New Delhi: The Publications Division, Government of India, 1964.

————. *Visit to America*. New York: The John Day Company, 1950.

PALMER, NORMAN D. *The Indian Political System*. Boston: Houghton Mifflin Company, 1961.

Report of a Study Group set up by The Indian Council of World Affairs. *India and the United Nations*. New York: Manhattan Publishing Co., 1957.

SHASTRI, LAL BAHADUR. *Speeches of Prime Minister Lal Bahadur Shastri*. New Delhi: The Publications Division, Government of India, 1965.

TALBOT, PHILLIPS, AND POPLAI, S. L. *India and America*. New York: Harper and Bros., 1958.

TRUMBALL, ROBERT. *As I See India*. New York: William Sloane Associates, 1956.

ARTICLES AND PERIODICALS

ANABTAWI, SAMIR N. "Neutralists and Neutralism," *Journal of Politics*, XXVII, No. 2, (May, 1965), 351–361.

APPADORAI, A. "India's Foreign Policy," *International Affairs*, XXV, No. 1, (January, 1949), 37–46.

————. "Why India Believes in Non-Alignment," *The March of India*, XIV, No. 10, (October, 1962), 11–12.

"Assembly Calls for New Disarmament Talks," *United Nations Review*, XI, No. 1, (January, 1964), 20–25.

"Attempt to Find Basis for Cease-Fire in Korea," *United Nations Bulletin,* X, No. 1, (January, 1951), 53–60.

BAJPAI, G. S. "India and the Balance of Power," in Charles H. Alexandrowicz. *The Indian Year Book of International Affairs.* Madras: University of Madras Press, 1952.

BANERJEE, P. K. "Certain Aspects of the United Nations," *Calcutta Review,* Vol. 139 (April, 1956), 11–16.

BARTON, SIR WILLIAM P. "India and World Politics," *The Fortnightly,* CLXX, (July, 1948), 96–98.

BIRDWOOD, LORD. "The United Nations and Asia," *Royal Central Asian Society Journal,* XLVII, Part III & IV, (July–October, 1960), 181–192.

BRECHER, MICHAEL. "Neutralism: An Analysis," *International Journal,* XVII, No. 3, (Summer, 1962), 224–236.

BROWN, MARY ALICE. "Some Aspects of India's Foreign Policy," *United Asia,* XII, No. 6, (1960), 493–498.

CLAIRE, D. S. "An Assessment of India's Foreign Policy," *Modern Review,* CVIII (September, 1960), 194–200.

"The Cost of Fear," *United Nations Bulletin,* IX, No. 8, (October 15, 1950), 392.

COUSINS, NORMAN. "Conversations With Nehru: Part I," *Saturday Review of Literature,* XXXIV, No. 15, (April 14, 1951), 19.

———, *ibid.,* (Part II), XXXIV, No. 16, (April 21, 1951), 7–124.

"Current World Economic Problems," *United Nations Bulletin,* XI, No. 5, (September 1, 1951), 202–204.

ELDRIDGE, P. J. "India's Non-Alignment Policy Reviewed," *Australian Outlook,* XIX, No. 2, (August, 1965), 146–157.

"Enforcing the Peace," *United Nations Bulletin,* IX, No. 2, (July 15, 1950), 46–47.

"Failure of A Mission to End Kashmir Deadlock," *United Nations Bulletin,* IX, No. 7, (October 1, 1950), 310–314.

FALLS, CYRIL. "Leading 'Third Force' Candidates," *The Illustrated London News,* CCXXXVII (October 8, 1960), 598.

"Financial Situation Considered by General Assembly," *United Nations Review,* X, No. 6, (June, 1963), 6–11.

"Financing of United Nations Operations in Congo in 1960," *United Nations Review,* VIII, No. 1, (January, 1961), 34–35.

FONTERA, RICHARD M. "Anti-Colonialism As A Basic Indian Foreign Policy," *Western Political Quarterly,* XIII, No. 2, (June, 1960), 421–432.

"The Foreign Policy of Mr. Nehru," *Round Table,* No. 176 (September, 1954), 363–368.

FORRESTER, DUNCAN B. "After Nehru," *Parliamentary Affairs,* XIX, No. 2, (Spring, 1966), 208–217.

"Fresh Effort for Kashmir Settlement," *United Nations Bulletin,* X, No. 6, (November 15, 1951), 253–259.

"Further Effort Endorsed for Kashmir Demilitarization," *United Nations Bulletin,* XI, No. 11 (December 1, 1951), 442–443.

"General Debate—Twentieth Session," *United Nations Monthly Chronicle,* II, No. 10, (November, 1965), 71–145.

GHOSH, BIRENDRA. "Revision of United Nations Charter," *Vigil,* XII (March 11, 1962), 122–34.

GLAZEBROOK, G. DeT. "The Middle Powers in the United Nations System," *International Organization,* Vol. 1, No. 2, (June, 1947), 307–315.

GREGORY, ROBERT G. "The Friendly Neighbor: India's Stand in the UN on African Issues During 1963," *AICC Economic Review,* XVI (June, 1964), 26–31.

HARRISON, SELIG S. "Troubled India and Her Neighbors," *Foreign Affairs,* XXXXIII, No. 2, (January, 1965), 312–330.

HAUSE, E. MALCOLM. "India: Non-Committed and Non-Aligned," *Western Political Quarterly,* XIII, No. 1, (March, 1960), 70–82.

"India and Pakistan Reply to Statements on Proposals," *United Nations Bulletin,* X, No. 7, (April 1, 1951), 319–323.

"India-Pakistan Question," *United Nations Review,* XI, No. 3, (March, 1964), 5–11.

"India the Uncommitted," *The Economist,* CLXXXVIII, August, 1958), 541–542.

"India's Foreign Policy," *The Fortnightly,* CLXXXII, (July, 1954), 8–12.

"International Cooperation Year in 1965 Called for by Assembly," *United Nations Review,* X, No. 2, (February, 1963), 65–66.

KAMATH, M. Y. "India at the United Nations," *United Asia,* IX, (September, 1957), 225–229.

KARUNAKARAN, K. P. "India and the United Nations," *The March of India,* X, No. 10, (October, 1958), 7–9.

"Kashmir Demilitarization Agreement Possible," *United Nations Bulletin,* XI, No. 9, (November 1, 1951), 350–351.

KHAN, RAHMATULLA. "Financial Problems of a U.N. Peace Force," *AICC Economic Review,* XV, No. 21, (April 7, 1964), 27–28.

KONDAPI, C. "Indian Opinion of the United Nations," *International Organization,* V, No. 4, (November, 1951), 709–721.

LALL, ARTHUR S. "Change and Continuity in India's Foreign Policy," *Orbis,* X, No. 1, (Spring, 1966), 91–105.

———. "The Asian Nations and United Nations," *International Organization,* XIX, No. 3, (Summer, 1965), 728–748.

LEVI, WERNER. "Behind Nehru's Foreign Policy," *World,* I, No. 11, (April, 1954), 24–30.

———. "India Debates Foreign Policy," *Far Eastern Survey,* XX, No. 5, (March, 1951), 49–52.

———. "Indian Neutralism Reconsidered," *Pacific Affairs,* XXXVII, No. 2, (Summer, 1964), 137–47.

———. "Necrology on Indian Neutralism," *Eastern World,* XVII No. 2, (February, 1963), 9–11.

———. "The Evolution of India's Foreign Policy," *Year Book of World Affairs,* 1958, XII, 115–132.

MAHADEVAN, T. M. P. "India's Policy of Non-Alignment," *The Indian Year Book of International Affairs,* Charles H. Alexandrowicz (ed.). Madras: University of Madras Press, 1952, 89–105.

"The Major Problem: Disarmament," *United Nations Review,* VII, No. 6, (December, 1960), 6–9.

MATHUR, R. N. "United Nations and World Peace: India's Contribution," *Indian Journal of Political Science,* XIX (April–June, 1958), 124–128.

"Measures to Repel Armed Attacks," *United Nations Bulletin,* IX, No. 2, (July 15, 1950), 65–70.

MEHTA, G. L. "India in World Affairs," *Vital Speeches,* XXI, No. 18, (July, 1955), 1322–25.

MEHTA, SWADESH. "The Organization of an International Force," *International Studies* (New Delhi), Vol. VII, No. 2, October, 1965), 205–227.

MUDALIAR, A. RAMASWAMY. "India's Foreign Policy," in *Nehru Abhinandan Granth: A Birthday Book.* Editorial Board. Allahabad Journal Press, 1949.

MUKHERJEE, HARIDAS. "The Politics of Non-Alignment," *Modern Review,* CXIII (February, 1963), 156–158.

NAIK, J. A. "India in World Affairs," *United Asia,* XVI (July–August, 1964), 229–234.

NAIR, N. P. "Non-Alignment: History, Ideology, Prospects," in *Outside the Contest,* Karunakaran, K. P. (ed.). New Delhi: Peoples Publishing House, 1963.

———. "Non-Alignment in World Affairs," *India Quarterly,* XVIII, No. 1, (January–March, 1962), 28–57.

NEHRU, JAWAHARLAL. "Changing India," *Foreign Affairs,* Vol. 41, No. 3, (April, 1963), 453–465.

"Noble Motives," *The Reporter,* XXI, No. 8, (November, 1959), 6.

"Off White Elephant," *The Economist,* CCII (February 10, 1962), 495–496.

PALMER, NORMAN D. "The Afro-Asians in the United Nations," in *The United States and the United Nations,* Gross, Franz B. (ed.). Norman: The University of Oklahoma Press, 1964.

———. "India Faces A New Decade," *Current History,* Vol. 40, No. 235 (March, 1961), 147–152.

———. "Indian Attitudes Toward Colonialism," *Orbis,* I, No. 2, (Summer, 1957), 211–236.

———. "India's Foreign Policy," *Political Quarterly,* XXXIII, No. 4, (1962), 391–403.

———. "India's Position in Asia," *Journal of International Affairs,* XVII, No. 2, (1963), 126–141.

————. "The United States and India," *Current History,* XXVIII, No. 161 (January, 1955), 43–50.

"Pandit Nehru's Foreign Policy," *The Economist,* CLIX, (July–December, 1950), 272–273.

PANDIT, VIJAYA LAKSHMI. "India's Foreign Policy," *Foreign Affairs,* XXXIV, No. 3, (April, 1956), 432–440.

"Peace-Keeping Operations: Committee Hears Statements," *United Nations Monthly Chronicle,* III, No. 11, (December, 1965), 72–76.

"President of India Sees United Nations Giving Conscience to World Community," *United Nations Review,* X, No. 7, (July, 1963), 51.

RAI, K. B. "India's Attitude Towards the Revision of the United Nations Charter-1," *Foreign Affairs Reports* (India), XIV, (June, 1965), 83–88.

————. "Indian Attitude Towards Revision of the United Nations Charter-11," *Foreign Affairs Reports* (India), XIV, (July, 1965), 106–112.

RAJAN, M. S. "Indian Foreign Policy in Action, 1954–56," *India Quarterly,* XVI (July–September 1960), 203–236.

RAMARAO, T. S. "India and the United Nations," in *The Indian Year Book of International Affairs,* Alexandrowicz, Charles H. (ed.). Madras: University of Madras Press, 1952, 246–257.

RAMU, P. S. "Policy of Non-Alignment: Has It Failed?" *AICC Economic Review,* XIV, (April, 1963), 24–27.

RAU, SIR B. N. "India and World Peace," *The Nation,* CLXI, No. 25 (December 16, 1950), 629–632.

————. "What Asia Can Give the World," *Vital Speeches,* XVII, No. 15, (May 15, 1951), 468–470.

"Report on the Congo: Implementation of Council Resolution and Further Exchanges of Messages," *United Nations Review,* VIII, No. 4, (April, 1961), 11–15.

ROSINGER, LAWRENCE K. "India in World Politics," *Far Eastern Survey,* XVIII, No. 20, (October, 1949), 229–233.

RUSSET, ALAN DE. "An Understanding of Indian Foreign Policy," *International Relations,* I, No. 11, (April, 1959), 543–556.

SAHA, SISIRRANJAN. "A Re-Appraisal of Non-Alignment," *Calcutta Review,* 175 (April, 1965), 17–23.

SCALAPINO, ROBERT A. "Neutralism in Asia," *American Political Science Review,* XXXVIII, No. 1, (March, 1954), 49–52.

"Security Council Adopts New Formula For Kashmir Settlement," *United Nations Bulletin,* X, No. 8, (April 15, 1951), 396–404.

SETALVAD, M. C. "India and the United Nations," *India Quarterly,* VI, (April–June, 1950), 107–129.

SOWARD, F. H. "The Changing Balance of Power in the United Nations," *Pacific Affairs,* XXVIII, No. 4, (October–December, 1957), 316–327.

STOLLE, JANE. "Purse String Diplomacy at The U.N.," *Nation,* Vol. 194, No. 3, (January 20, 1962), 44–47.

SUD, USHA. "Committee on Information from Non-Self-Governing Territories," *International Studies,* VII, No. 2, (October, 1965), 311–336.

"Summary of Main Decisions of the Resumed Fifteenth Session of the General Assembly," *United Nations Review,* VIII, No. 5, (May, 1961), 5–11.

"UNEF: Reorganization of Forces in Gaza and Sinai," *United Nations Monthly Chronicle,* III, No. 3, (March, 1966), 12.

"U.N.O. Secretariat," *The Eastern Economist,* VII (December 20, 1946), 997–998.

"The United Nations: A Symposium on Its Organization and Structure," *Seminar* (March, 1962), 10–42.

"United Nations—The One Hope for Peaceful Cooperation," *United Nations Bulletin,* VIII, No. 11, (June 1, 1950), 455–457.

"U Thant of Burma Appointed Acting Secretary-General," *United Nations Review,* VIII, No. 12, (December, 1961), 16–20.

NEWSPAPERS

The Christian Science Monitor.
The Hindu Weekly Review.

India News.
The New York Times.
The Times (London).

UNPUBLISHED MATERIAL

VARMA, SHANTI NARAYAN. "India's Policy in the United Nations with Respect to the Maintenance of International Peace and Security," Unpublished Dissertation, Department of Political Science, Columbia University, 1952.

Index